QUOTABLE CUOMO
THE MARIO YEARS

The consummate quote book for Cuomo fans and foes

compiled by
Brian Meyer and Mary Murray
Cover Photo by Joe Traver for the New York Times

DEDICATIONS

From Brian Meyer:

To my many dear friends who made this project possible by helping me to walk through the painful doors of the present ... and especially to Shelly, who helped me unlock the door to the future. ILY.

From Mary Murray:

This book is dedicated to the two most important people in my life; my son, Kevin, and my mother, Elizabeth ... and to my deceased father, Melvin, whose untimely death led me, in a roundabout way, to the path of journalism as a career.

ACKNOWLEDGMENTS

Many people helped to make this book a reality. Our sincere appreciation is extended to the following individuals: Loretta Yearke, Anna Finkel and the entire crew at Yearke Graphics for their expertise and patience; the crews at Partner's Press and Printing Prep; John Hardiman for devising our cover concept and Cathy Linden for taking the authors' photographs.

Our thanks also goes to John DeMerle and Randy Bushover from WBEN Radio, who graciously agreed to tape Mario Cuomo's monthly *Ask the Governor* program. The WBEN newsroom and our interns were helpful in keeping their eyes and ears open for new "Cuomoisms." We also thank WIVB Television for its contributions.

Margaret "Peggy" Ray, the governor's Western New York liaison, was helpful in tracking down the texts of several Cuomo speeches.

Finally, we thank Joe Traver for contributing insightful photographs to our lively text.

THE COMPILATION TASK

Reporter Brian Meyer has covered more than 100 Cuomo functions over the past decade in Buffalo, Albany, Niagara Falls and many other communities. Many of the quotes and anecdotes contained in this book come from news conferences, public hearings, ribbon-cuttings, plant tours and other events that Meyer covered over the years.

Other quotes come from public speeches made by the governor, his statewide radio show, media interviews and dozens of other sources. Authors Meyer and Mary Murray engaged in a comprehensive, seven-month research mission, reviewing many broadcast transcripts, periodicals and books, including the *Diaries of Mario Cuomo* (Random House, © 1984) and *Mario Cuomo, A Biography* (by Robert S. McElvaine, Scribner's Sons, © 1988).

Finally, some Cuomo fans and foes contributed entries to this book. The authors are grateful to everyone who helped to make this project a reality.

CONTENTS

INTRODUCTION

"Which one is Cuomo?"
The flustered reporters eyed the two men who walked briskly through the lobby of a downtown Buffalo hotel.

"I think he's the tall one," said one reporter. "But is that how you pronounce his name? Is it Quo-mo? Or Como? You know, like the singer?"

But before the mystery could be pondered any further, New York's lieutenant governor introduced himself.

It was a bone-chilling winter day in 1982 and Mario Cuomo was thinking ahead to November. He wanted to be governor.

But while many New York City-area residents were familiar with the man who has been labelled the Hamlet on the Hudson, most upstate residents had never heard of Cuomo. Not to mention folks in Kansas and California, Maine and Missouri.

It would have been pure folly, then, to predict on that cold morning back in 1982 that within a few years, Mario Cuomo's political stock would skyrocket faster than perhaps any other Democratic leader in the nation. He became the party's most articulate spokesman on economic issues, launching blistering attacks on the Reagan and Bush administrations. His impassioned messages prompted many Democrats to try to nudge Cuomo into running for president.

But a state deficit crisis in 1990 and 1991 caused Cuomo's popularity back home to plummet to all-time lows.

For this reason, the authors of this book agonized over the merits of this offbeat project. During our seven months of intensive research, we wondered aloud many times whether the climate was suitable for a breezy, anecdote-driven book that attempted to chronicle Cuomo's stands on literally hundreds of issues.

We decided to go with our gut instincts, figuring that both fans and foes of New York's high-profile governor would find this a useful resource book as well as an entertaining armchair companion.

And by the way. It's Quo-mo. Not Como.

BUDGET BRAWLS

"I've seen trouble, and there's never been trouble like you are about to observe."

This was the sobering message Governor Cuomo delivered to civic and business leaders days before he released his "disaster" budget in late 1990. His warning was no exaggeration. A multi-billion dollar shortfall transformed a traditionally topsy-turvy fiscal process into a chaotic tug-of-war. The end result was the longest budget stalemate in state history.

■■■

"We cannot avoid all of the pain, but we can use this ordeal to inspire changes that can help lead us to a new era of progress... We don't have any money; we don't have any other options. Let's shock everybody... let's tell everybody the whole truth."

– 1991
(State of the State address)

■■■

This fiscal turmoil paralyzed the state budget process. Cuomo and the State Legislature engaged in marathon finger-pointing, each side blaming the other for the stalemate.

"At the moment, I see no end to the impasse," Cuomo said in April, 1991, days after a new spending plan was slated to take effect. "History is repeating itself. So is a failed process."

– 1991

■■■

Cuomo renewed his call for a new state law that would withhold the paychecks of all elected state officials (including his own) until leaders could agree on a budget.

"If you haven't done your work, you shouldn't be paid. A painter who shows up and puts his brush down, you don't pay him."

– 1991

When the governor proposed sweeping layoffs as one strategy for coping with the budget morass, employee unions, elected leaders and many rank-and-file citizens assailed the plan.

"In the private sector (layoffs) happen every day. You have a million more people out of work in one year. It happens in the private sector. It doesn't happen in government. That's one of the reasons people are so upset. They live lives where they can be fired. Where their businesses can go bankrupt, where their jobs can be eliminated. And then you come to government and government gets all upset at the notion that it might have to cut back. The regular taxpayer doesn't understand why public employees should say 'we should have jobs for life, even if all the rest of you are getting laid off, we should be preserved. And how should we be preserved? By raising your taxes.' It doesn't make sense."

-1991

■ ■ ■

Cuomo challenged local governments across the state to turn the nagging deficit woes into an opportunity for streamlining their operations.

"You can make of this moment an opportunity to tighten your belt, to lose some weight, to get stronger, to get smarter about how you spend, to break an old habit that says 'all we have to do is throw money at the problem and we'll solve it.'"

-1991

■ ■ ■

Cuomo's perennial metaphor comparing New York to a family nudged its way into the budget brouhaha. The governor called for responsible belt-tightening, warning there could be some pain.

"...Our state must approach this problem by sacrificing some of what we hoped to do for our family this year."

-1991

"People don't want new taxes. I don't want new taxes, and (Erie) County Executive Gorski doesn't want new taxes. That means we have to cut back."

–1991

■ ■ ■

When someone challenged the governor to defend his decision to veto millions of dollars in additional aid for education, he explained it in terms that the average person could understand:

"It was Monopoly money. It was phony money. You would have never seen it, anyway."

–1991

■ ■ ■

Joe Traver for The New York Times

The governor's fiscal policies have frequently been the focus of protestors, including students and faculty members in the state university system.

■ ■ ■

But the governor on occasion would try to provide some levity to the state's somber fiscal outlook and its chaotic budget process. While speaking to a group assembled at the Erie Community College City Campus in downtown Buffalo, Cuomo made mention of an anecdote that was told earlier in the presentation by a local attorney.

"It was a pleasure to hear Arnold Gardner's interesting story about that student quarterback who put 16 and 22 together and got 39. For those of you who are wondering what happened to that fellow, he succeeded. He got himself a fairly well paying job. He is in Albany at the moment, working on the budget!"

–1991

■ ■ ■

When State Comptroller Edward Regan asked for a $10,000 salary increase in the same season that elected leaders where grappling with the deficit crisis, Cuomo rejected the request.

"There's no way you can ask to lay off thousands of people just before Christmas and ask others to surrender five days' pay ... then turn around (and ask for a raise) ... I was surprised to see the letter, to put it mildly."

–1991

■ ■ ■

As the state budget stalemate dragged into its second month, causing severe problems for New York City and many other localities, the governor called on legislative leaders to reach an accord.

"If the leaders keep playing chicken with one another, the rest of us are liable to wind up dead ducks."

–1991

■ ■ ■

"Now it's the legislators' turn at bat, and they have to step in the box ... They can't be so afraid of beanballs that they don't come to the plate."

–1991

■ ■ ■

"It is now time to make up your mind. There is no more advantage in tactical delay. There is only catastrophe."

At one point, legislative leaders struggled unsuccessfully to conclude the budget talks before the arrival of an important weekend; Senator Tarky Lombardi, chairman of the powerful Senate Finance Committee and a Syracuse Republican, wanted to be out of Albany in time for his daughter's wedding.

"That's terrific. I wish his daughter had gotten married in April."

-1991

■ ■ ■

When the Legislature talked about chopping from the payroll a number of high-paid state agency jobs, the governor made it clear two could play that game.

"That sounds very much like micro-management of the agencies by the Legislature ... I think if you look at your own budget in the Legislature, you'll find at least as many high-paying jobs that you can get rid of ... Just as you have a constitutional right to review my agencies, we have a constitutional right to look at your legislative budget."

-1991

■ ■ ■

"It is now three weeks since I presented the budget. You've heard an awful lot of name-calling, cursing, unhappiness; all of it coming from groups that ... acknowledge you should really reduce spending to some extent, but then don't say reduce the part of the spending that applies to me."

-1991

■ ■ ■

Cuomo assailed state lawmakers for attempting to make spending cuts in "vital" areas such as the state prison system. During an appearance on Albany radio station WAMC's *Capitol Connection* show, the governor launched another attack on the Legislature's fiscal priorities.

"Across the board, mindless cuts ... They just say 'Take 1 percent wherever you get it.'"

-1991

■ ■ ■

"Why should the taxpayers be held hostage? All you're doing is punishing taxpayers for no good reason, just throwing their money down the sewer ... For the ninth straight year, they've made it apparent that this is a body that abhors any political difficulty. They don't want to make tough decisions."

-1991

■ ■ ■

"They have retreated from the field and are now in separate trenches, waving political flags at each other. The recession in this country is getting worse and ... the legislators are acting as though it's not real."

-1991

■ ■ ■

During a candid one-on-one interview in Albany with a reporter from a Buffalo radio station WBEN, Cuomo accused the Legislature of hurting school districts and localities.

"They blew it. They might just as well have taken the dollars and put a match to them. What for? Well, because they felt the lateness gave them some leverage. You have an assemblymen and maybe a senator or two from the Western New York delegation who told representatives from the city of Buffalo 'Don't worry, the later, the better for you, because you'll get more money ... To use irresponsibility as a weapon, that's no way to govern. I'm disappointed."

-1991

■ ■ ■

Both the Assembly and the Senate insisted on financing many of their proposed budget restorations by downwardly revising Cuomo's spending estimates. This angered the governor.

"It's the old game. You just bounce up the revenues, bounce up the expectations, and spend it. When the state goes into deficit, it's the governor that they nail."   -1991

■ ■ ■

During his monthly statewide radio call-in show, Cuomo tried to make it easier for listeners to understand the fiscal maneuvering in Albany. He borrowed a scene from Tinsel Town to describe lawmakers' alleged propensity to overspend, then suggest that their budget figures are more accurate that the administration's estimates.

"It's very much like Big Julie in *Guys and Dolls*. Big Julie was the gambler, the tough gambler who was rolling dice with Frankie Sinatra in the movie. Big Julie is getting creamed in the dice game, so he decides to make a comeback. He's a tough guy. A hood. He reaches into his pocket and say (Cuomo lowers his voice and uses a street-smart dialect) now we play with **my** dice.' So he takes out his dice and Frankie looks at them and says 'there are no numbers on your dice, Big Julie.' And Big Julie says 'Dare are numbers, its gist that I'm da only one who can see 'em.' He rolls the dice and he says 'seven!' The Legislature is rolling the dice and saying seven. That's alright, except that nobody else can see the numbers."

-1991

■ ■ ■

Cuomo repeatedly ridiculed Senate Republicans for being hypocritical about their reputed desire to cut state spending.

"There is no question that they're taxers and spenders, and they always have been."

-1991

■ ■ ■

"They have done some truly stupid things with some of these cuts. No, not stupid - stupid means they made a judgment."

-1991

Midway through the unpredictable budget negotiations, the governor attended a dinner of the Legislature's Black and Puerto Rican Caucus. He defended his budget proposal, a plan that proposed $4.5 billion in painful cuts. Some argued the belt-tightening would hit minorities and the impoverished harder than other segments of the population. But Cuomo argued against plans to raise income, sales and corporate taxes. He warned it could drive employers out of the state.

"People you're trying to help you could actually destroy. You are jeopardizing the business that your children will have to work in."

-1991

■ ■ ■

During an interview in his Albany office with WBEN Radio's Brian Meyer, Cuomo talked about a protest held in Buffalo earlier in the month. Sign-toting demonstrators demanded that the governor cut the deficit by increasing taxes levied on corporations, rather than reduce funding for vital programs.

"We've redued (taxes) not to save corporations and make them wealthier, but to keep business here so that poor and middle class people will have a chance to work. You tax steel enough, and it will leave. You tax the automakers enough and they'll go somewhere else. It's fine to thump your chest and say 'we really hit those corporations hard, 'but you're going to be hitting the people who are working in those places if you drive them away. In the long run, this will cost you more money."

-1991

■ ■ ■

"I'm one of the most effective governors in the country at taxing the rich. I thought up taxes on the rich. Like the gains on real estate of a million dollars or more. So I know all about that ... But these people who are chanting in the streets of Buffalo, when they say 'tax the rich,' they're being deceptive. They want a 3 to 4 billion dollar tax. You can't get that from the rich. You can get a couple hundred million dollars, maybe. But all the rest comes from you, from me, from people making $11,000 a year."

-1991

■ ■ ■

In what some billed as a bid to dramatize the chaos caused by the state's budget deadlock, Governor Cuomo issued a sobering warning in mid-May. He said his Tax Department was going to run out of money for the postage it needed to mail tax refunds to 1.3 million residents.

"By Friday the Tax Department will be out of the money it needs to send you back your refunds. Think of it. The Tax Department will be broke."

(The refunds were ultimately mailed.)"

-1991

■ ■ ■

A wag once remarked that "The wages of sin are death, but by the time taxes are taken out, it's just sort of a tired feeling." During the winter and spring of 1991, Albany decision-makers were obsessed with talk about taxes; bickering of what strategies should be used to boost revenues and close the deficit. Governor Cuomo blasted a Legislature plan to impose a tax on petroleum products.

"I said the (petroleum tax) is the lemon of the year"

-1991

■ ■ ■

The bickering centered largely on whether the state should increase income taxes or go along with Cuomo's proposed 10-cent-a-gallon hike in the gasoline tax. At one point, Assembly Speaker Mel Miller of Brooklyn proclaimed the gas tax dead, prompting a caustic response from the governor.

"To say the gas tax is dead ... and substitute it with a (personal income tax hike) that is deader on arrival doesn't make a whole lot of sense."

-1991

■ ■ ■

But even though the 1990-91 state budget was agonizing for Albany decision-makers, Cuomo looked ahead to even bigger

problems. He noted the economic turmoil facing both the state and the nation and said of the just completed budget process:
"You think this was combat? Wait until next year."

-1991

■ ■ ■

In October of 1991, the governor warned of a budget deficit that could hit $500 million. He said it was obvious the economy was not rebounding as some had expected and he predicted if there was an upturn, the economy would probably stumble again before there was a full recovery.
"Call it a double dip, a double blip, call it double whatever you want. My guess right now is that we've not made a recovery."

-1991

■ ■ ■

Albany budget brouhahas were not born in 1991. State lawmakers and governors have long feuded about fiscal matters. In 1990, when Senate Republicans steadfastly refused to go along with the governor's plan for new taxes, he criticized the GOP.
"If (Republicans) sit there and stamp their feet and say unrealistic things beyond April 1, this state is in a disastrous fiscal predicament and everybody knows it and they know it."

-1990

■ ■ ■

"Spending is not bad. Spending may be absolutely essential. And the spending we have done, when I tell you it is not the highest in the nation, that is not to say I believe we would commit a sin if it were. Because what we spend on, we need to spend on, and maybe in some cases we should have spent more."

-1990

When Cuomo proposed delaying a $1.7 billion tax cut, the state Republican party mailed literature to businessmen who contributed to the governor's campaign, as well as newspapers and other 'opinion leaders.' The GOP even mailed fliers to 100 households on Pompeii Avenue, Queens, where the Cuomo family once lived. The slinger had a headline that screamed: "Mario Giveth and Mario Taketh Away." The governor's reaction?

"They're just being cute."

-1989

■ ■ ■

Cuomo reaffirmed his desire to delay the final phase of the income tax cut when he spoke on WSKG, a Binghamton public radio station.

"What I would suggest? Put it off for a year. Defer it. Don't abandon it, just put it off. You know you need the money now. You know you're short now."

-1989

■ ■ ■

"This decision is for the Republicans. If they insist on keeping the tax cut, and it's entirely up to them ... then they are denying their people $1.6 billion. And when they get the budget and when somebody raises his hand ... and says' 'Governor, we need more money for schools,' and that person happens to be a Republican, I will say to them, 'You gave it away. You had it but you didn't want to spend it on schools."

-1989

■ ■ ■

"Clearly, for a while, we will be unable to sustain the rates of spending growth of these past six years. The criterion of need - as distinguished from wants - will have to be applied even more stringently than before. First things must come first; programs that affect immediately the conditions of our peoples' lives before less urgent matters."

-1989

■■■

Creative taxing has often been the order of the day in Albany, as decision-makers struggled with strategies for raising revenue without inflicting too much pain. Governor Cuomo once hatched a plan for cashing-in on unredeemed pop bottle deposits. He noted his proposal would generate more than $80 million annually.

"The beverage industry has retained more than $360 million in unclaimed beverage container deposits since the bottle bill was implemented in 1983."

–1989

When legislative leaders on both sides of the political aisle rejected the governor's request for emergency deficit reduction powers, Cuomo lamented:

"I suspect this is not going to be the jolliest of Christmas seasons or Hanukkah seasons."

–1988

■■■

Budget cuts even occasionally raise the ire of Cuomo's clan. On his 56th birthday, Cuomo told reporters his wife was so angry at him over his attempts to slash aid for a state council she runs that she threatened not to buy him a birthday gift. He proposed cutting $500,000 from the state's Council on Children and Families.

"She was very unhappy, but businesslike. She said, 'Why did you do it to me?' I said, 'We didn't do it to you.'"

Cuomo then explained that he made his wife the same offer he made to state agency heads; if she could find a better place to cut, then he would consider it.

"She said, 'Good, we'll start with your birthday present.'"

–1988

Sharing the pain has been one of the governor's favorite phrases in dealing with annual budget quandries. Cuomo has also repeatedly stressed the need to set priorities.

"I'm all for zoos. If you're going to have animals, you better have zoos. (But ...) If the monkeys eat a banana that's a day old, it wouldn't be so terrible."

-1988

■ ■ ■

"I would prefer a system where (the state) gave local governments less, and gave them the capacity to raise their own revenues so that their people could make judgements as to what you want to pay taxes for and what you want to spend on. The government closest to the people is the best. Let them make more of the decisions."

-1987

■ ■ ■

Governor Cuomo warned public employees they might have to settle for smaller raises than they want so the state can pay for vital programs.

"Some needs are greater than other needs and over the next six or seven months we have to look for a tightening of our economy, a reduction in growth."

-1987

■ ■ ■

But Cuomo has prided himself in being a staunch friend of the unions. He has acknowledged his debt to the AFL-CIO for its early support of him when he ran for governor in 1982. Speaking to delegates at the union's state convention in Kiamesha Lake, Cuomo praised organized labor's accomplishments.

"Without the union movement, this country would not be as great as it is today."

-1988

■ ■ ■

"If all I did was balance the budget without finding ways to improve the conditions of people's lives - the middle class, the poor, the disadvantaged - then a balanced budget would become the emblem of hypocrisy. Government has to do more than make the books come out."

-1982

■ ■ ■

During his stint as the number two man in Albany, Lt. Gov. Cuomo once reflected on the stormy state budget process in his diary.

"Still no state budget, with less than a week to go. I like to think I would do it differently and better, if I were governor. I wonder if I'll ever know?"

-1981

■ ■ ■

THE GAME OF POLITICS ≣

Ask Mario Cuomo what he thinks about political consultants and he will tell you:

"I've never used any of them. I use Andrew, my family and some friends. I always did. That's how I won. It would be kind of silly to all of a sudden spend a fortune on pros when I did it with amateurs."

–1990

■■■

Upon accepting the Democratic nomination for a third term as governor, Cuomo proceeded to discuss his administation's perceived accomplishments.

"In this business, if you don't blow your own horn, there's no music."

–1990

■■■

"I've never had any grand (political) ambitions for myself. I didn't even aspire to be governor until very late in life because I didn't think I could ever do it. And when I suddenly found myself lieutenant governor, which happened virtually by accident, I was just a failed politician up until then. I've never desired anything more or thought about anything more"

–1990

■■■

"Words and phrases like 'conservative, liberal' may be unavoidable habits of our expression, but they are not useful as meaningful descriptions of the complex forces with which our policies must contend."

–1987

■■■

"We often campaign in poetry, but then we're always required to govern in prose. In the end, much of the campaign rhetoric proves to be an impediment to appropriate policy-making."

–1987

■ ■ ■

Confidence is critical in any successful political campaign. Cuomo admitted his main weakness when he ran for New York mayor in 1977 was that he considered most of his opponents better candidates than himself. But he said his confidence level increased when he ran for governor.

"That's what made me strong in the campaign. I looked around and said 'None of these people are as good as I am.'"

(Cuomo's political stock skyrocketed when he defeated Ed Koch in the Democratic gubernatorial primary and later defeated the wealthy GOP candidate Lew Lehrman in a Rocky-like conquest for the state's top post.)

-1985

■ ■ ■

"I don't like the national attention as much as I like being governor, frankly ... This I enjoy ... I enjoy the work ... I like piling up ideas ... I can do it all day long because I like it so much. If you didn't love it, you couldn't do it. If somebody hired me to do this work, I wouldn't be able to do it."

-1985

■ ■ ■

He mesmerized 26 million viewers and, in one powerful speech, forged his image as a presidential contender. Some said Cuomo's half-hour address filled with poetic appeals was the only "fresh thing" to emerge from the 1984 Democratic presidential convention in San Francisco."

"In fact, Mr. President, this nation is more a 'tale of two cities' than it is a 'shining city on a hill.' Maybe if you visited more places, Mr. President, you'd understand. Maybe if you went to where thousands of unemployed steelworkers who wonder why we subsidize foreign steel while we surrender their dignity to unemployment and to welfare checks, maybe if you stepped into a shelter in Chicago and talked with some of the homeless there, maybe, Mr. President, if you asked a woman who'd been denied the help she needs to feed her children because you say we need the money to give a tax break to a millionaire or to build a missile we can't even afford to use, maybe then you'd understand. Maybe, Mr. President, but I'm afraid not."

-1984

■ ■ ■

"...To succeed we will have to surrender small parts of our individual interests to build a platform we can all stand on, at once, comfortably, proudly singing out the truth for the nation to heal, in chorus, its logic so clear and commanding."

-1984

■ ■ ■

"The intellectual process in campaigns ... at least until you get into the booth on election day ... is terribly superficial and at time cynical. It can be depressing to hear people tell you over and over that while they prefer you on the merits, they want to be with the winner. And the more that's felt, the stronger it becomes; it feeds on itself."

-1982

■ ■ ■

During a strategy session at a restaurant, the governor talked finances with William Stern, his chief fund raiser, and other political operatives. For the primary, Stern had helped to raise $1.7 million from six thousand contributors, many of them small contributors. An example was a construction worker who gave the Cuomo camp a check for $2.50. Now, Stern said the "big money" people were calling. Unlike the construction worker, these potential heavy-hitting contributors wanted to meet the candidate and be assured that their gift would be appreciated. Cuomo suggested they could meet with him at a Post Inauguration party. But Bill Haddad, his campaign manager, looked less than pleased. Cuomo amended his stand.

"Make it an act of faith. What the little people did, the big people can do. Tell them 'you got to believe.'"

-1982

Joe Traver for The New York Times

Candidate Cuomo gets a kiss of support from Gail Ciroalo, a representative of the Civil Service Employees Association. Cuomo was on the 1982 campaign trail, stumping for votes in Western New York.

In his diaries, Cuomo recalled how a friend from Queens telephoned him to say one of the power brokers who had supported Ed Koch in the gubernatorial primary was ready to sit down with Cuomo. Shaking his head, Cuomo said to his friend, "all the money that went for Koch that I criticized every bit of it is reaching out for me." When the friend reminded Cuomo the power broker could deliver a sizable chunk of the Jewish vote, Cuomo responded:

"This guy was born wanting things. On his way out of the womb he was looking to do business with the nurse. I know he could deliver a lot of things. Tell him he can go deliver, but just stay away from me."

–1982

RUNNING FOR GOVERNOR

Cuomo campers called him "Pop-up Pierre." It was clear right from the start of the 1990 gubernatorial campaign that the three-way faceoff for the state's most powerful elected post would be a colorful contest, if not a close one. Republican candidate Pierre Rinfret provided most of the comic relief, frequently showing up unannounced at Cuomo functions and triggering lively encounters. Rinfret's unorthodox and unpredictable campaign strategies prompted Conservative Party candidate Herb London to chastise the GOP for failing to embrace his candidacy.

During a visit to the General Mills plant on the outskirts of downtown Buffalo, Cuomo was confronted by an uninvited Rinfret.

"Politics is a little bit silly here. I mean it's obvious that if he were the major candidate he says he is, he wouldn't be popping up from the bushes to get his face on television, right? He'd go to the people of the state and he'd talk to them. He has $15 million. He can buy television ... Pop-up Pierre. This isn't the first time he has done this. He popped up from the bushes before."

(Cuomo then drew laughter when he suggested that Rinfret's face would probably next pop-up from a Wheaties box inside the General Mills plant.)

-1990

■■■

During a lively television debate, Rinfret, a former professor, told the governor that if he had been in his economics class, Cuomo would have flunked. Without missing a beat, Cuomo replied that if he had taken Rinfret's economics class, he should have been committed.

-1990

■■■

During a speech to campaign workers at the Empire State Plaza, Cuomo made it clear he wanted a clean election, devoid of mudslinging.

"I'm tired of people pointing fingers and doing commercials with Pinocchio nose and saying 'She's a drunk and he's a dope addict.'

What I'd like to see the campaign become is a kind of instruction to the whole United States of America."

-1990

■ ■ ■

When asked if he planned on seeking re-election in the spring of 1990, Cuomo replied:

"Unless you have a better job for me than governor, chances are I will try to do it as governor."

But is there is a better job?

"I doubt it very much."

-1990

The Breakfast of Champions: *Cuomo proudly displays a commemorative cereal box given to him during a 1990 visit to a General Mills plant in Western New York.*

■ ■ ■

When Cuomo ran unsuccessfully for the Democratic nomination for lieutenant governor in 1974, he recalled later that the decorum of the courtroom had not prepared him for the hurly burly of the political soapbox.

"I was too professional."

-1986

■ ■ ■

Cuomo was talking to Republican gubernatorial candidate Andrew O'Rourke on a radio show. O'Rourke came out swinging in the campaign and Cuomo couldn't forget. "Andy, you started this campaign calling my son corrupt, calling me corrupt and calling me a liar."

-1986

■ ■ ■

Because Cuomo had never won an election, he was dismissed by many party leaders as a loser when he launched his gubernatorial campaign in 1982. He was viewed by some as a cerebral politician; one who spent far too much time agonizing over all sides of an issue. In fact, skits put on by reporters in Albany and New York City on occasion depicted the lieutenant governor as Hamlet. Upon hearing this, Cuomo hinted that perhaps there was another Shakespearian character that could be used to highlight the foibles of his political foe, Ed Koch, Cuomo was referring to Polonius, the wind bag in *Hamlet*.

-1982

■ ■ ■

Cuomo found himself participating in the same parade as GOP opponent Lew Lehrman. The families encountered one another on Madison Avenue. The lieutenant governor picked up three-year-old Peter Lehrman.

The elder Lehrman said, "Peter, tell the lieutenant governor who's going to be the next governor."

The tyke proudly pointed to his dad. Cuomo responded: "But Peter, you don't even know me!"

-1982

■ ■ ■

On his way to the parade, Cuomo heard somebody shout; he thought the person was calling his name. He raised his hand to wave, only to realize that the voice belonged to a gentleman who was calling to a passing girl.

"Now I am getting egocentric."

-1982

■ ■ ■

Earlier in the fiery gubernatorial faceoff, Cuomo appeared at a debate in the ballroom of the Shearton Center. He and Ed Koch were preparing for a pivotal duel-of-the-tongues. The audience was comprised of 600 business people and other opinion leaders. In his diaries, he recalled the scene.

"I walked in the back door of the crowded ballroom and an extraordinary thing happened. Some people began applauding... As I moved toward the main table, where Koch, Mayor Lindsay and some university presidents were sitting... the applause grew. By the time I got to the main table and reached out to shake hands with the mayor, the applause was really quite rousing. At a debate that hadn't even started! All we needed was the *Rocky* theme in the background. I knew Ed was unhappy..."

-1982

■ ■ ■

Koch later won the coin toss and chose to let Cuomo open so the fiesty New York City mayor could close the debate. Seconds after he called the coin, Cuomo grabbed the microphone and yelled:

"No wonder he's for casino gambling!"

(Cuomo later recalled that the quip immediately set the tone of the debate. He said he could tell Koch was even unhappier than he was when the crowd greeted Cuomo with a thunderous applause.)

-1982

■ ■ ■

When Governor Hugh Carey backed away from a pledge to support Cuomo's candidacy for governor, Cuomo protested the perceived betrayal, paying an in-person visit to his boss. He angrily conveyed his feelings of betrayal. Stung, Carey started to get out of his chair.

"Sit down, Hughie... or I'll knock you right on your ass."

The governor leaned back into his chair.

-1982

PRESIDENTIAL POLITICS

"(I have) no plans and no plans to make plans (for a presidential run). I'm not a potential candidate. I'm not a make-believe candidate."

- 1991

■ ■ ■

No Cuomo quote was more repeated in 1991 than his "no plans and no plans to make plans" assertion. As Democrats scrambled to find a viable candidate to challenge George Bush, who was enjoying unprecedented popularity in the wake of the nation's victory in the Persian Gulf War, the eyes of America were riveted on Cuomo. People incessantly asked "Will he or won't he?" The governor often times appeared exasperated. During his statewide radio call-in show, he lamented:

"It appears to be impossible to use any language that would end the question forever.... If you did rule it out, if you said 'No sir, I won't, I've made up my mind, that's it; you know what (reporters) would write then? 'I wonder if he's got a Mafia uncle in the closet. I wonder why he's ruling it out. You cannot win. That's what I learned in 1987, and if you can't win, at one point, you say 'Forget about it, I'm not gonna play.'"

- 1991

■ ■ ■

"If I did say convincingly that under no circumstances would I ever run, that would be so unreasonable a position that people would say, 'There must be something in his closet.' Now I wouldn't mind if they said it was a 28-year-old blonde, but they don't say that. They say, 'His uncle's Mafia'."

- 1991

■ ■ ■

During the summer of 1991, Cuomo said there is no way he could run for president and be governor if he had to confront the nagging problems he encountered in his home state this year. "There's no way you could have done this and anything else... (Imagine) how difficult it would be even to think about something like that... I kind of smile when I hear legislators say, 'We all know he's running for president.' Can you imagine trying to run for president under these circumstances, when you're working seven days a week, fighting, scheming?"

- 1991

■ ■ ■

Speaking to a visibly disappointed U.S. Conference of Mayors in Hyannis, Massachusetts, Cuomo edged further away from jumping into the 1992 presidential fray.

"I don't think my state has ever needed a governor more than it does now. That is the commitment I have made."

- 1991

■ ■ ■

"It's flattering that this comes up, and I thank you... But I don't have any special magic with the words or the ideas. I gave a speech once in 1984, and it was well-received at the convention... Why? What resonated with the people was not Mario Cuomo; they don't know me. At least they didn't know me in 1984. What is important is the message."

- 1991

■ ■ ■

"It's the message. And if you agree with the message, and you think it's a useful message, then there are better instruments for its delivery, I assure you. Younger, smoother. There's all kinds of stuff out there. Persona you can get, if we can agree on the message."

- 1991

■ ■ ■

Cuomo went on the tell the mayors:
"What role will I play? I'll do anything you ask me to do - *as governor*!"
(The convention hall then erupted in laughter.)

- 1991

■ ■ ■

There are all sorts of people who speak better than I do, who have better enunciation, who are younger, taller, stronger..."

- 1991

■ ■ ■

During an appearance on CBS' *Face the Nation*, a *Washington Post* reporter noted that other prominent Democrats have been open and candid about their levels of interest in running for president. Cuomo was asked why he was unable to be just as open and candid.

"I've been more open and candid than any of them. Nobody knows better than you that I've had only one answer for eight years. The fact that you're irritated with the answer is inexplicable to me. I have said for eight years the same thing. I have no plans to run for president. Now why that should be so difficult to understand... why I shouldn't be able to say to E.J. and to others in this country 'Look, I know a lot about the issues and I have a contribution to make by recommending some things that ought to be done... But I don't have any plans to be president. Why must you plan to be president? Especially if you're in a party chalked full of talent."

- 1991

■ ■ ■

One of the underlying questions in the 1992 presidential sweepstakes was whether any Democrat could beat George Bush. Cuomo insisted the president was vulnerable, despite his popularity.

"What else have they done besides win a war?"

- 1991

■ ■ ■

During an interview with Buffalo radio reporter Brian Meyer in Albany, Cuomo talked about some political pundits' views that Bush was invulnerable.

"Remember that some said Bush couldn't win the presidency in the beginning of 1988. He was a loser. He was a wimp. Remember the magazine covers? 'Bush the Wimp.' A few weeks ago, he was 91 in the polls. So having been so fooled by history in '88, what makes you think you can be so sure about history in '92? Of course, a Democrat can win!"

- 1991

■ ■ ■

In the same interview with WBEN Radio, the governor expressed the belief that a popular defense policy, in an of itself, cannot win a presidential election.

"Harry Truman, after he won the war, was a big favorite. Months later, he was way down in the polls. Winston Churchill saved the world. Three or four months later, he was down. Kohl was 90 in the polls last year. Now he's at 39. Why? Because the unification of East and West Germany produced economic trouble. Economic trouble is what people can relate to most. Jobs. Interest rates. Business. Whether you have health insurance. The things that most make it to your table, make it to your house, make it to your bed when you're all alone and you're trying to get to sleep and you're worried about how to take care of the kids. That's what makes the difference."

- 1991

■ ■ ■

"In 1988, Nobody figured on the Willie Horton thing or the Harbor (pollution in Boston), or the Pledge of Allegiance... Nobody ever expected they would turn this thing around in three lousy commercials."

- 1991

■ ■ ■

How can you say that you can't win? That this man is too hard to beat? The prize is worth wanting. And if Democrats have nothing to offer, they shouldn't win."

- 1991

■ ■ ■

Cuomo once told editors of a newspaper in Middletown, New York that the federal government has boosted taxes 14 times since Ronald Reagan was sworn in as president in 1980.

"That's Reagan-Bush. Nobody knows that. People haven't caught on. Once they make the association, Washington will have a lot to explain."

- 1991

■ ■ ■

"President Reagan smiled at us for eight years and said everything is great, the economy is terrific, you can have the biggest military machine, you can have the biggest tax cuts in history and you didn't have to pay the price... Now we realize we have a huge debt around our throats, Japan and West Germany are ahead of us, the economy has gone to seed."

- 1990

■ ■ ■

You have excellent candidates... Bill Bradley, Al Gore, Parkin, Saunders, Mitchell... and any of these people can serve as excellent candidates. What we need now are ideas, and there are plenty of them."

- 1991

■ ■ ■

"More important, frankly for the Democrats than finding new players to play at being president, is finding new plays."

- 1991

■ ■ ■

"I've said over and over that I think Al Gore would make a good candidate."

- 1991

■ ■ ■

Cuomo also had glowing things to say about Paul Tsongas who became the first Democrat to declare his presidential aspirations in the 1992 race. The governor called Tsongas "a subtle, intelligent, principled" man. Cuomo pooh-poohed claims that Tsongas' presidential chances were weakened by widespread perceptions that he was just another Michael Dukakis; a liberal, Greek-American from Massachusetts. Cuomo replied caustically:

"Anyone who (thinks that) is probably a narrow-minded, shriveled-up Republican-type.

- 1991

■ ■ ■

"The Democrats are late. Why are they late? Because you had a war. You couldn't, in the middle of the Persian Gulf controversy, be Bill Bradley and stand up, or Al Gore and say 'Hey look, forget about the war! I'm telling you the economy is in terrible trouble and we need to do something.' Everybody knew the economy was in trouble, but you couldn't talk about it until the war was over. The president is popular. What will the president's slogan be when he runs? You know what it is going to have to come to? 'I won the war, the other guy's a bum.' What else can he say? Can he say he's produced more jobs? Ten million Americans are out of work. Can he say 'I was truly the education president'? He cut education. Can he say 'I won the war on drugs'? Go to any city in the United States and answer that question for yourselves. He can only say 'I know we have problems; I don't have any plans to deal with them...' I'll tell you on the merits - on these issues, this campaign could be easy for the Democrats."

- 1991

■ ■ ■

Days after Cuomo's gubernatorial victory over Pierre Rinfret and Herb London, U.S. Housing Secretary Jack Kemp predicted the Democrats would choose Cuomo to run against George Bush. Said Kemp: "I think he will be the candidate. I think we should relish it, and it will be a wonderful debate between Mario and George." Cuomo's reply:

"I like Jack even when he's playing... I'm used to debating Republican economists. I just finished one with Pierre Rinfret, and they all sound alike... One hopes the houses that Jack builds, for the sake of those who have to live in them, are better than his supply-side theories."

- 1990

In the fall of 1989, Buffalo television reporter Rick Pfeiffer asked the governor about another political run. Cumo interrupted him.

"How could you possibly say that they would need you as president in 1992, unless you've got some fixation, some egocentric desire to hoist yourself to the top for whatever reason... and I don't suffer from that problem."

(Pfeiffer then replied: "Uh, governor, I was referring to another bid for the governor's race.")

- 1989

Cuomo was highly critical of the negative tone that embraced the 1988 presidential election between Democrat Michael Dukakis and George Bush.

"If there's anything about this election that strikes me, that I find debilitating, it's the harshness, the crassness, the negativism. (The theme was) you do what you have to do to win. On the way there, you gouge out eyes, you lie, you cheat. I find that disconcerting."

- 1989

Cuomo once said he thinks many power brokers have ignored for too long the messages of the Rev. Jesse Jackson, who sought the Democratic presidential nomination in 1988.

"We have to start treating Jesse like everyone else. No more condescension. No more double standards. Give him the dignity he demands, and all the scrutiny we demand of others. Only then can white Democrats legitimately compete for black voters in the primaries and still have their heavy participation in the general election, without which we lose. Only then are you credible when you say, 'we white office-holders are the ones who can actually deliver what Jesse talks about,'"

- 1991

■■■

Buffalo news anchor Bob Koop asked Cuomo about many people envisioning a broken democratic convention - one in which Simon, Dukakis, Gephardt, and Jackson cancel each other out and party leaders turn to Cuomo to bail out his party and the nation.

Cuomo responded by saying, "You can't reject the people that you have tested and try somebody who is not tested. If your party wasn't good enough to produce a winner and a champion in the normal process, than you're not good enough to be president, that's the way the American people would see it."

The governor's predictions in the 1988 presidential sweepstakes proved too far off-base. He told Buffalo television anchor Bob Koop, of WIVB, Channel 4 that whoever wins the Democratic presidential nod will be the next occupant in the White House.

"Dukakis, if he's the candidate, sweeps. Jackson, if he is the candidate, sweeps. Absolutely. No, I'm telling you. It will be a Democratic landslide."

- 1988

■■■

"I'll never be president... I won't get a chance because the Democrats are going to be in place for eight years and by then I will be a vague whisper of a footnote in the book of New York State life."

- 1987

■■■

In an interview published in Time Magazine, Cuomo talked about his lack of interest in becoming president.

"I see that job as a burden, not as an opportunity... Let this cup pass."

- 1986

■ ■ ■

During an Albany news conference in June, 1986, reporters were dogging the governor about speculation that he might run for president two years up the road. His response suggested that he had no interest, but he refused to emphatically state that he wouldn't run.

Cuomo remains non-committal in his bid for the White House. "Look, I'm not sending hints out because I don't intend to send hints out and when I do, it won't be a hint. I'll stand up and say I changed my mind."

- 1986

■ ■ ■

"I don't think I have what it takes (to run for president). I don't think I have the persona."

- 1985

■ ■ ■

During a lively exchange with members of the National Press Club in Washington, Cuomo was asked about his presidential aspirations, and his chances of winning.

Reporter: "There are those who say that Mario Cuomo, should he seek the presidency, does not have the ideas and a philosphy that is transportable to other parts of the country, particularly the south, the midwest and the west."

Cuomo: "Yeah, but I'm terrific in Hoboken!"

- 1985

■ ■ ■

If I run (for governor in 1986, I don't plan to run (for president) in 1988. How could I run a race for governor in 1986, which ends Jan. 1, 1987... You're dead broke, you've just got beaten up for three months, then what do you do? Turn around and start raising money for a presidential race and start running around the country? How do you do that?"

PERSONAL INSIGHTS

"The most effective thing I am able to do on stage is make people laugh."

■ ■ ■

Indeed, Cuomo's keen wit is rivaled only by his ability to communicate oftentimes complex philosophical concepts in plainfolks terms. Of course, he sometimes borrows from other visionary thinkers. He once quoted Aristotle's rule for success: decide what you want to do and do it. He once confided to a *New York Times* reporter that it was really his mother's rule for success.

"But no one would listen unless I said it was Aristotle."

■ ■ ■

Known for his aggressive play on the basketball court, Cuomo reported in October of 1991 that he was nursing a "boo-boo" he got while playing the sport.

"Over the weekend, I had an injury. I got some stitches in my arm and got a slightly chipped elbow," he told an Albany radio station. "It's called a boo-boo."

He went on to explain that he was only "defending" himself in the game against some state troopers. He refused to point any fingers when asked which trooper was responsible for the "boo-boo." But he did chuckle and say: "All you need to do is look for transfers."

–1991

■ ■ ■

A young man named Jeff once called the governor's monthly radio program, a show that is broadcast in all parts of the state. They were talking about lofty education issues when the caller informed the governor that he was at a pay phone, getting ready to go on a skiing trip with his girlfriend.

Cuomo: Jeff, you're calling me instead of seeing your girlfriend?
Jeff: "Well, I…"
Cuomo: Jeff, don't go to your girlfriend, go to a psychiatrist!"

"Governments are not the most efficient vehicles in the world, especially if they don't have pressure on them."

-1991

■ ■ ■

"I don't like speeches. I don't like making them. I don't like preparing for them."

-1990

■ ■ ■

Cuomo spent a season playing minor league baseball. He once talked about the game being a uniquely American tradition that, unlike any other sport, binds generation to generation.

"It's a little leaguers' game that major leaguers play extraordinarily well; a game that excites us throughout adulthood. The crack of the bat and the scent of horsehide on leather bring back our memories that have been washed away with the sweat and tears of summers long gone... Even as the setting sun rushes the shadows past home plate."

-1989

Joe Traver

Number One Fan. Governor Cuomo displays a jersey given to him during a visit with Buffalo Bills owner Ralph Wilson.

■ ■ ■

During an interview with Buffalo television station WIVB, Cuomo talked about being in the public eye.

"I think the most difficult thing for me in the public life is to give up your privacy. This isn't easy talking on television. Normal people don't sit around their living rooms and say 'Well, Bob, let me tell you about myself.' I don't particularly like it, to be honest with you. On the other hand, it comes with the job."

–1988

■ ■ ■

"I had no youth… It was just school and the store – always the store. It never changed – only the displays in the windows changed. But I never did what most kids did. My time was always occupied, but I never had a youth like most kids. It was very uninteresting; it would only bore people."

–1984

■ ■ ■

When his mother, Immaculata, was busy working in the family store, young Mario would be in the back room, entertaining himself by taking a long, hollow piece of dry pasta and small dried peas. The two made for versatile grocery store armament.

"You could use them as peashooters until the end of the macaroni got soggy from the moisture of your mouth, and then you had to break off a piece. So your peashooter was constantly getting shorter and shorter, until you ran out of peashooter. It should only happen to the Pentagon!"

–1984

■ ■ ■

While a student at St. John's Prep, many considered Mario to be "cocky, arrogant and brash." One vivid example: the dean saw the student standing in a second floor hallway, holding a lighted cigarette. Smoking was a flagrant violation of college rules, which banned smoking above the first floor. The dean directed Cuomo to report to his office at once.

"Why?"

"Because smoking here is against the rules," the dean responded coolly.

"Did you see me smoking? Is there a rule against carrying a lighted cigarette?"

"Do you mean to tell me that your were not smoking?"

"No, Father, I'm not going to say that I wasn't, but I'm not going to say that I was, either. I have shoes on, but I'm not walking."

On several occasions during his meteoric political career, the governor reflected on his brief stint as a major league baseball player. He often remarked that he never really wanted the life of an athlete badly enought to make good.

"It was fun, but I needed something more... There had to be more to life than playing ball. I felt I had to do something else. I didn't know what, but I knew - I thought - that I had to look beyond center field for it."

-1984

Hitting upon the same theme, the governor has explained his interest in politics by citing the opportunity to help the homeless, the poor and other segments of society.

"I didn't come into this business to be an accountant. I came into this business to help people."

-1986

"A lot of intelligent people tell me not to do something; I think about it and take their advice. But the popular opinion of intelligent people can be off. When you have a powerful instinct, you ought to go with it."

-1986

■ ■ ■

Someone once said "You don't stop laughing because you grow old; you grow old because you stop laughing." Regardless of the location, the event or the subject at hand, one can be sure that when Mario Cuomo is the speaker, it will be laced with at least a dash of humor. He has some favorite jokes that he tends to recycle, putting slightly different spins on them to fit the occasion. His tales often serve two purposes; he can make a biting point without sounding harsh. And he can get the attention of his audience.

Speaking at an education forum in New York City, Cuomo dug into his encyclopedia of funny bone-ticklers.

"This subject brings to mind a number of stories... A mother tries to wake up her son for school. 'You've got to get up,' the mother tells her son. 'I don't want to get up,' he answers. 'Come on, you've got to.' 'Give one good reason why,' the son says. 'I'll give you two reasons,' the mother says. 'One, you're 40 years old, and two, you're the principal.'"

–1985

Joe Traver for The New York Times

A reflective Mario Cuomo reads in his office in the state capitol.

■ ■ ■

Loosening up this crowd of 1,000 educators and the Big Apple leaders, the governor was now ready to veer into a more serious theme. He served up another tale.

"The rains came, and the water was rising so rapidly that people fled from their homes. They got out any way that they could – boats, rafts. The water was up to their waists. The last large rowboat came back for one person, a priest. 'Father, if you don't get into this rowboat, you're going to drown.' 'Oh no, I have faith. I'm sure God will save me.' The last helicopter comes by. 'Father, you're going to drown; climb up the ladder.' 'Oh no, I have faith, God will take care of me.'

"The priest drowns and goes to heaven, where he asks 'Oh, God, do you know me?' 'Of course I know you,' God answers. 'You're one of my loyal, honest, faithful servants.' 'Then why did you let me drown?' 'Father, what could I do?' God asks. 'I sent you a rowboat. I sent you a helicopter.'"

Then for a moral of the story, delivered by New York State's premier storyteller.

"Help is available all around us. It's just up to us to realize it and make the most of it."

–1985

■ ■ ■

In the midst of a conversation the governor is having with an elderly woman from Queens, Cuomo's press secretary sneezes just as the woman begins to speak. The woman explains that this is a yiddish sign that the person talking is telling the truth.
Cuomo turns to his aide and says: "Next time, see if you can sneeze while *I'm* talking."

–1986

■ ■ ■

In describing his pet dog, Ginger, Cuomo once said:
"A mutt like me. But prettier."

–1982

Joe Traver for The New York Times

An 85-year-old Niagara Falls resident plays an old Italian game with Governor Cuomo in which fingers are thrown and guessed. The match occurred when the governor visited a Niagara County senior citizen center.

■ ■ ■

But Cuomo's reflections can be just as stone serious as they can be humorous. During an interview in New York magazine, the then-lieutenant governor talked about the need for compassion in society.

"(A)ll this harshness, anger, selfishness of the past few years is false. We move through cycles. In the sixties, we went overboard on love – the hippies, the Great Society. Everything should be done in moderation. So there was a reaction – you had to be tough. Stop caring about the poor. Compassion was weakness. But I think people are tired of that now. It's more natural to be compassionate."

–1986

■ ■ ■

"The idea of family is the bedrock in which my political philosophy rests."

-1982

■ ■ ■

In his diaries, the governor recalled how an astrologist once sent him a horoscope that predicted he would die on election day.

"I don't know if she meant it literally or figuratively. Just in case she means it literally, I think I'll vote early."

-1982

■ ■ ■

In his revealing diaries, Cuomo reflected on his first uphill battle to become governor.

"Again today I was reminded that perhaps the greatest danger of all in a campaign like this one is forgetting why you are doing it – or at least why you should be doing it. The temptation is to measure everything as though victory is …. the most important thing. It is the only thing. A bad day in the press; an important rejection, a slumping poll and the spirits sag, frustration, depression, sometimes even anger set in… because we forget that what is really important is the effort: doing it well, trying it well, living it well."

-1982

■ ■ ■

FAMILY

When a New York City television station questioned the Cuomo family's use of state airplanes and helicopters, the governor went on the defensive. He dealt with the issue in his statewide radio call-in show.

"We have had an Air Force since 1931 and there has never been an administration in the history of this state since then that has been tougher on the use of those planes than I have been... I noticed Channel 2 referred to Matilda being on the flight. What they failed to tell people is that she had worked free for eight years. I'm talking about working day and night, not as some dilettante. She gets nothing, no stipend, no salary. And she doesn't want anything."

(Matilda serves with the Council on Children and Families.)

–1991

■ ■ ■

Immaculata Cuomo is among the most frequently mentioned names when the governor makes speeches. He often evokes the words and wisdom of his mother to bring some plain-folks perspective to lofty issues.

During a 1990 get-out-the-vote rally in the Buffalo Convention Center, Cuomo told supporters his administration could have easily neglected to disclose a nagging state deficit until after the election. He even hinted that if his mom was running his re-election campaign, the fiscal woes would have probably been kept hushed until after voters had trekked to the polls.

"My mother does not believe in lying. She believes in not telling you."

–1990

■ ■ ■

When Cuomo was running against Ed Koch for mayor of New York City, it was the 'Son of Sam summer' and many people were clamoring for the death penalty. Many years later, Cuomo told supporters in Buffalo that his mother warned him his tough stand against the death penalty was going to lose him the election. He told her he would rather lose than sell out his convictions. Immaculata paused, giving careful thought to her son's dilemma.

"Then she said 'Here's what you do. You tell 'em you gonna give 'em the electric chair. After the election...'" (his mother then made an ancient Italian gesture, flicking the bottom of the chin with two fingers, throwing out the hand, palm open, essentially saying to H--- with them.)

-1990

■ ■ ■

One of Cuomo's favorite "momma" stories on the speaking circuit involves her lifelong dream of seeing her son become a judge. To the hardy laughs of audiences, Cuomo has often reflected on his mother's reaction to news that he was named secretary of state.

"Oh, that'sa nice. When you gonna be judge?"

A few years later, he became lieutenant governor.

That'sa nice. When you gonna be judge?"

"Whattaya mean, Ma? I'm the *governor!*"

She responded: "Stupido: Stupido: How long is governor?"

"Four years, Ma."

"How long is Supreme Court judge?"

"Life, Ma."

"Who's stupid, me or you?"

■ ■ ■

Some have suggested the governor's proclivity to interject stories about his mother and other family members borders on gimmickry. But few would argue that the tales help to make Cuomo one of the most appreciated speakers on the national political circuit.

During a visit to Buffalo in the mid 1980s, the governor met with members of the *Buffalo News* editorial board. Before the editors even had a chance to probe some burning issues, Cuomo was once again talking about "Momma" and how he recently walked in on her when she was riveted to the television set. She was watching *The Thorn Birds.* He recalled how she was sitting on the edge of her chair, aghast at the steamy plot.

'There'sa girl. She tooka her clothes off and a priest, oh, my God..."'

"Ma, then why are you watching it?"

"Oh, it'sa so good!"

-1985

■ ■ ■

Cuomo's references to his father are much less frequent than the anecdotes about his mother. But they can be every bit as colorful. Take the day he was speaking to The Partnership, a group of influential Wall Street businessmen.

"You know, I have a lot in common with you in that my father lost his business. Yes, a stockbroker jumped out of a window and landed on his push cart."

-1985

■ ■ ■

Even though Cuomo resides in an elegant 40-room governor's mansion, he prides himself in the fact that his values haven't changed; values given to him by immigrant parents.

"If I brought home a report card that didn't have (A's), my father would slap me. At the time, I thought it was harsh and cruel and stupid and unfair and I probably resented him. You get to be a little bit older, you understand why he did it and the point he was trying to make. Education was everything to him. So what did my mother mean? (She) was the embodiment of the best values I've ever learned. No cardinal, no pope, no school teacher could teach me more about values than she did and she couldn't give a speech, she couldn't write a letter. When she heard I was going into politics, she and my father were just surprised and frightened. They thought politics was for rascals and scoundrels. That's all they knew about it!"

-1988

■ ■ ■

"In my neighborhood where I was raised and in our grocery store; everybody was a different color, different ethnicity - alot of them spoke different languages, but they were all the same; they were all the poor, struggling into the middle class."

-1988

■■■

During a revealing interview with television anchorman Bob Koop of Buffalo's WIVB-TV, Channel 4, Cuomo talked extensively about his family. He said that never in his parents' wildest dreams would they have thought that their son would become the state's most powerful elected leader.

"...These people who couldn't speak the language, who had no friends, who had no influence, who knew nothing about politics, who had no money... (to think that) someday their son would get to be the governor like the Rockefellers, like the Harrimans, like the Kennedys. You could come from South Jamaica, Queens with nothing and start late after you're forty, have no career, have the establishment all against you, and get to be the governor. Of course they're astonished, and so am I."

-1988

■■■

"We started in a poor neighborhood. We became middle class. And now I have people pressing my pants. So I've gone all the way up the ladder and met all kinds of people in the process."

-1988

■■■

But Cuomo's references to his family are not always as light-hearted and oozing with sentimentality. On occasion, situations have arisen where he has bristled at suggestions that the Cuomo family have acted in their own self-interest. When the governor's wife, Matilda, encouraged state officials to fund a cancer registry study done by her brother, Cuomo was miffed. He said it was "terribly unfair" to suggest that Matilda had anything but the best interests of New York residents in mind.

"(She) has voluntarily contributed extraordinary amounts of her time and energy... to improving health care and education in New York... Any suggestion that she would do anything for any reason other than to help the people of this state, would be both inaccurate and terribly unfair."

(Cuomo's defensive statement added that both Matilda and her brother had been "active volunteers in the fight against cancer for many years.")

-1988

■ ■ ■

Matilda speaks in glowing terms of her husband as she criss-crosses the state - and the nation - on a myriad of awareness missions. But she once confided that she thinks her husband would be better off if he didn't always have such a severe outlook on life.

"He still takes everything so seriously. Maybe it's our upbringing. We had to struggle so hard."

-1986

■ ■ ■

One such serious moment came during his baseball days. The youthful Cuomo was playing a game in Tifton, Georgia. He had a tiff with the catcher. Perhaps "tiff" is too weak of a word, because Cuomo became so incensed that he swung around and punched the catcher in the face. He was asked about the incident during an interview on *60 Minutes*, and he admitted the altercation did occur "on a very bad day and a very weak moment. Someone said something offensive, so I rose up in righteous indignation and, yes, I hit him in the mask."

-1985

■ ■ ■

The concept of family has long been fodder in Cuomo's speeches. One of the most memorable speeches of the governor's career - and a speech that catapulted him into the national political limelight - was his moving address to delegates attending the 1984 Democratic Convention in San Francisco.

"We Democrats believe that we can make it all the way with the whole family intact. We have more than once. Ever since Franklin Roosevelt lifted himself from his wheelchair to lift this nation from its knees; wagon train after wagon train - to new frontiers of education, housing, peace. The whole family aboard - constantly reaching out to extend and enlarge that family. Lifting them up into the wagon on the way. Blacks and Hispanics, people of every ethnic group and native Americans - all those struggling to build their families and claim some small share of America."

-1984

■ ■ ■

Mario Cuomo first used the concept of family at a speech he delivered in a state fair in Syracuse in 1981. And family was the central theme of his 1983 inaugural address.

"And no family that favored its strong children - or that in the name of evenhandedness, failed to help its vulnerable ones - would be worthy of the name. And no state, or nation, that chooses to ignore its troubled regions and people, while watching others thrive, can call itself justified.

"We must be the family of New York - feeling one another's pain; sharing one another's blessings, reasonably, equitably, honestly, fairly - irrespective of geography or race or political affiliation."

-1983

■ ■ ■

Those who have been fortunate enough to get behind-the-scenes glimpses into Cuomo's everyday family life are struck by its down-home, earthy quality. One correspondent recalled a Sunday morning scenario in which the governor sat in the kitchen, dressed in jeans, entertaining his 11-year-old son, Christopher, with stories of his athletic heroics.

"You probably won't believe this, but I played on a minor-league baseball team where we wore Bermuda shorts instead of knickers... I've got pictures. Matilda, where's the scrapbook?"

-1982

■ ■ ■

The governor's oldest son, Andrew, has been prone to sharing with the press his father's traditonal values. When Andrew was 24, he told a *New York Times* reporter he and his dad never really had that proverbial talk about the birds and the bees.

"Let's put it this way - I'm still waiting for my talk on sex. My father used to tell me whenever I went out with someone, 'just remember that the girl you're going out with tonight is somebody else's sister.'"

-1982

■ ■ ■

Indeed, Mario Cuomo is not shy about admitting when he is wrong, especially when it comes to family. He once sadly recalled Parents' Day at St. John's Prep, where he attended school.

"You had to bring your parents to the school... but everybody in the school was Irish - an occasional Italian, but high-class Italian - son of a doctor, son of a lawyer. And I had to say 'bring mama and papa from the grocery store?' They wouldn't understand a word. So I decided not to ask them to come. To save them from embarrassment. There has never been a judgment in my life that I have rued more."

-1982

■ ■ ■

"When I think of all the people around us whose lives have been spent dealing with drug addiction or crime or abortions or nervous breakdowns, I feel almost guilty about our good fortune. That's the case generally where I'm concerned. I've always had the feeling that I've been given much more than I deserve and much more than most others and that most of my life should be spent trying to give something back. It's important to be even. Although I've never been able to figure out exactly why."

-1981

THE ABORTION DEBATE

"I accept the Catholic teaching on abortion... the question is, why am I required to ask for a constitutional amendment (prohibiting abortion), which I know would not work, which nobody wants, which you can't describe, and which Presidents Bush and Reagan who promised it to you, never produced? And politically, I'm saying, I'm not required to do that. I'm not required, because I'm a Catholic, to make everybody else Catholic, to make everybody else Catholic by passing a law. I'm not required to use politics to achieve what the church cannot achieve through the pulpit."

-1990

■■■

New York City's Catholic Auxiliary Bishop Austin Vaughan who is assigned to St. Patrick's Catholic Church in Newburgh, called Cuomo a "Sunday Catholic" and likened him to a Nazi soldier who may have thought slaughtering Jews was wrong but supported his government's rights to do it.

Invited by New York reporters to respond. Cuomo said: "I'm not going to call him any names. I'll leave that to the bishop... I think it hurts what he represents and is supposed to represent, which is tolerance, gentility and understanding. Does any bishop, any rabbi, any citizen have the right to curse a politician, curse them even to hell? In this wonderful country the answer is yes. "The right I'm defending is the right of this bishop to curse any politician he wants, and every woman to make her own judgment under the Constitution as to whether or not to have an abortion. It is the same freedom, sometimes used less elegantly than other times."

-1990

■■■

Responding to a statement made by Catholic Auxiliary Bishop Austin Vaughan that said Cuomo risks going "straight to hell if he dies tonight" for his pro-choice stance on abortion, Cuomo said "the freedom that permits a bishop to curse a politician to hell is the same as the freedom that permits a woman to choose abortion... I think my soul will be judged like yours and like the bishop's, by a higher and wiser power than the bishop... I am the governor of all the people and I think it is not my place to try to convert all of them to Catholicism and to insist that they live the way I believe I privately should live."

-1990

■ ■ ■

Cuomo predicted any effort to kill Medicaid funding for abortion would fail again in the State Legislature, even though the United States Supreme Court upheld the rights of states to restrict abortions.

"I don't think Webster vs Reproductive Health Services will change anything. The Medicaid question is here every year, and this state does not believe that the right to an abortion excludes poor women. This state won't buy that."

-1989

■ ■ ■

Cuomo suggested President Bush hasn't championed a constitutional amendment against abortion the way he has against burning the flag because it remains too volatile an issue..

"He (Bush) can't deal with a constitutional amendment for abortion, but the flag – he's right out there at the monument with the soldiers."

-1989

■ ■ ■

Cuomo insisted that most women he talks to feel abortion should be their choice and that nobody should make it for them.

"I am finding that even the most conservative women who believe that abortion is wrong say, 'that's my judgment, you can't make a rule for me because it's not your place'."

-1989

■ ■ ■

While the Supreme Court's decision won't affect New York State's historic willingness to pay for Medicaid abortions, he lamented the effect it will have on the entire nation.

"God forbid we get to the point where we let this go to 50 different states for 50 different judgments," he said.

■ ■ ■

Cuomo said that the recent decision by the Supreme Court was a political decision rather than a judicial one because of the clear intent of the Reagan Administration to mold a Supreme Court based on conservatism. He suggested every Supreme nominee at one point faced the abortion "litmus test," ruling out anyone who was not a conservative.

"That's like picking an umpire to call balls and strikes the way you want."

−1989

■ ■ ■

After giving a speech in Tucson, Arizona, Cuomo responded to an editorial published by the magazine "America" regarding women's position on abortion.

"I felt presumptuous talking about the terrible, hard judgment women make with regard to abortion. I do. I am very uncomfortable with having to make decisions about abortion. I do think there is an element of the absurd or incongruous in men making laws about something they can never experience, pregnancy. I think every male should feel uncomfortable making such judgments. But we've been doing it a long time, both in the church and in the government. Certainly I knew that when I chose public life."

−1989

■ ■ ■

Saying "God should not be made into a celestial party chairman." Cuomo defended the pro-choice decision of vice presidential candidate Geraldine Ferraro, a Catholic congresswoman from New

York at a speech he gave at the University of Notre Dame. The speech was later deemed a benchmark on the role of religion and politics.

-1984

■ ■ ■

Cuomo's personal beliefs on abortion were evident when he delivered one of his most renowned speeches. He gave the address at the University of Notre Dame.

…"When should I argue to make my religions value your morality? My rule of conduct your limitation? What are the rules and policies that should influence the exercise of this right to argue and promote?"

…"I believe I have a salvific (sic) mission as a Catholic. Does that mean I am in conscience required to do everything I can as Governor to translate all my religious values into the laws and regulations of the state of New York or the United States? or be branded a hypocrite if I don't?"

…"I accept the church's teaching on abortion. Must I insist you do? By law? By denying you your Medicaid funding? By a constitutional amendment? If so which one? Would that be the best way to avoid abortions or to prevent them?"

-1984

■ ■ ■

NATIONAL ISSUES

Referring to the Persian Gulf War, Cuomo said that the Republicans had erred by "holding themselves out as the party of war, which is the way it sounds."

"This country doesn't want somebody who burns candles to the god Mars," he continued. "We want somebody who can win a war that is forced upon us and made inevitable and can win the peace just as effectively."

-1991

■ ■ ■

Although Governor Cuomo had high praise for President Bush and the American troops for handling the war "superbly well," he said the country's exhilaration would be multiplied if the White House could prove it was equally adept at making peace.

"We've proven that we're very good at war, and you need to be," he said. "Imagine the joy this country would experience if we could prove now we're very good at peace, which we haven't done yet.'

-1991

■ ■ ■

"Cheap and foolish" were the words leveled by Cuomo against the New York Conservative Party when they ran a full-page advertisement in the New York Times ridiculing New York Senator Daniel Patrick Moynihan's vote against the Persian Gulf War. The ad read "Where was Pat Moynihan when Americans needed him?"
"It's a shame that magnificent debate should be desecrated now by tawdry politics that reveal conservative and radical Republicans at their very worst. What the conservatives have revealed is that what they're best at is negativism. Their whole philosophy is a sort of Willie Horton campaign technique." (referring to the Republicans' widely-criticized presidential campaign tactics used against Massachusetts Governor Michael Dukakis).

-1991

Cuomo said President Bush had ill prepared the public for the Persian Gulf War and its aftermath.

"It's a mistake to pretend you can have a new world order without having first a new American order."

Cuomo added that he thought Bush was "being too cute" by half-acknowledging certain domestic needs and then by largely ignoring them.

"You made a choice – bankers before babies."

–1991

■ ■ ■

During an interview on CBS' *Face The Nation*, Cuomo was asked who was right on the Persian Gulf war, the Democrats or the President?

"I would say the President did a very right thing by going to Congress and asking their permission; remember we thought he wouldn't? So he was right going to Congress. The Congress said it was right to go to war. Since the Congress told him he should go to war, he did the right thing by winning it, and the people who did it most right of all were the men and women from my state and every other state who went there willing to sacrifice their lives – and some of them did. They were the most right of all."

–1991

■ ■ ■

Cuomo was asked if he thought the President should have continued the war until Saddam Hussein was destroyed.

"It's easy to be Monday morning quarterback ... if you vote to go to war you must add a coda- if you fight them, we must destroy Saddam Hussein, no nuclear, no biological, no chemical, no army. Put him away. If you're going to kill people including your own, then make sure you get rid of Saddam Hussein. That we never did. That was wrong! ... You've got to find a way to neutralize him ... God forbid you now announce that you have to have a second war to do what you should have done the first time. We have to now be smart enough to take care of Saddam Hussein, which we should have in the war and that was my position before it even started. So that, we didn't do right".

-1991

■ ■ ■

Cuomo insisted there is still no clear cut answer as to whether going to war was the best move. Cuomo said, "Because you win a war doesn't mean that the war was the best decision."

Recalling that the United States won World War I and World War II, Cuomo asked "Would the society have been better off without any of these wars? How are you to say "No, we absolutely needed the wars?' Did you absolutely need the Civil War? You'll never know."

-1991

■ ■ ■

According to Cuomo, President Bush never fully informed the American People as to why the United States forces were in the Persian Gulf. "That probably suits Bush's purpose. I think it was better politically from the President's point of view to say to the American people we're there because Kuwait is entitled to independence than to say we're there for oil. The truth is, we're there for oil."

-1990

■ ■ ■

Cuomo told the *New York Post* he wasn't impressed with the Democratic Leadership Council's efforts to shed the party's liberal image in order to appeal to more voters (the group consists of Arkansas Governor Bill Clinton and Georgia Senator Albert Gore, Jr.)

"I didn't hear these people say that government has an obligation to take care of those people who can't make it in the free enterprise system because they're too old, too weak or too ill. Without that, we're not the Democratic Party. I didn't hear them talk about that. It's like they think they have to do penance for sins we Democrats never committed and, to that extent, they are giving solace to our enemies."

-1991

■ ■ ■

"We have a federal debt so large people can't even remember its size, and we have never been weaker economically or in most other ways."

-1991

■ ■ ■

In a speech to the Guardians of the Jewish Homes for the Aging in Los Angeles, Cuomo talked about Iraq's invasion of Kuwait and efforts by the United States and others to reverse it.

"You would negotiate something that gets them out of Kuwait for the most part, leaves them maybe a little bit of the water, leaves them a little bit of the oil, and then puts in a United Nations task force to go over the whole question of chemical weapons...and this movement toward nuclear capacity." (by Iraq).

-1990

■ ■ ■

"I think you need a force like the United Nations that becomes real to keep peace in the world. Can't ask the United States to go rushing off every time there's a problem. Frankly, we don't have the wealth any more to do it."

-1990

■ ■ ■

During a speech in Hyannis, Mass. before the nation's governors, Cuomo insisted the Bush administration has done little to respond to the social curses, such as 23 million illiterates "who can't read the instructions on a bottle of poison."

-1991

■ ■ ■

"The simplistic approach that says to be a liberal, you must constantly give money even if you don't have it, even if you're going to go bankrupt, is stupid. All of my fight was for a liberal agenda.

But it would have debilitated our economic base, it would have cost us so much credibility in the investment community that in the long run, poor people would suffer. We are the state, not the federal government. The federal government can create money. It can run deficits. In the state, there is no source of wealth other than the wealth we generate out of our own tax system. That's where we get the money for wheelchairs."

-1989

■ ■ ■

"President Reagan and Reagonomics were not absurd conceptually. If you had spent a little less money for defense, but still increased defense spending, if you had spent less money in tax cuts but had a tax cut; if you said you don't have to balance the budget in three years, you have to balance the budget in ten or thirteen years, Reagonomics would have been fine."

-1988

■ ■ ■

"I think it would be a mistake to be fooled by Soviet Leader Mikhail Gorbachev's talent, his charm and his candor. No matter how well he dresses it up, and he is a charming man, the Soviet's philosophy hasn't changed."

-1987

■ ■ ■

"This is the time to deal with the Soviet Union. The Soviets are vulnerable, in their economy and in their selves. There's a survival mentality now, and the people want more. Soviet Leader Mikhail Gorbachev didn't invent glasnost (openness) because it was an inspiration; it's a response to an observed need of the population. So far, though, they haven't paid a significant price for glasnost - but they will. You can't give people a few liberties and expect their appetites to be satisfied. Of course, there's a flip side. Many people feel threatened by changing a system of guarantees even if those guarantees add up only to bare survival. So Gorbachev may not last."

-1987

■ ■ ■

Cuomo once discussed the Iran Contra hearings during a Democratic fundraiser in Indianapolis. "I think, frankly, it is that yearning for inspiration, for edification that produced the phenomenon we witnessed during the Iran Contra hearings. So badly did we want a true believer, a hero, in the early days of the hearings, many of us were fooled into overlooking the fact that the men we chose to hoist onto our shoulders (those involved in the Iran Contra scandal) were in the process of destroying one of our most important values of all – the rule of law."

-1987

■ ■ ■

Referring to revelations that Lt. Col. Oliver North circumvented the legal limits of his authority and the fact the former National Security Council official was viewed by many as a hero, Cuomo told the crowd: "Think of it, every mad man who ever usurped a people's rightful power started by saying 'I'm better than the law.' "

-1987

■ ■ ■

Speaking in Springfield, Illinois before the Abraham Lincoln Association, Cuomo compared today's modern day economic conditions to conditions more than a century ago.

"In Lincoln's time, one of every seven Americans was a slave. Today, for all our affluence and might, despite what every day is described as our continuing economic recovery, nearly one in every seven Americans lives in poverty, not in chains – because Lincoln saved us from that – but trapped in a cycle of despair that is its own enslavement."

-1986

■ ■ ■

"This government calls itself conservative. It has the largest budget and the largest deficit in the history of the universe. Since they invented counting, there has never been a government or a budget like this."

-1985

■ ■ ■

The difference between Democrats and the Republicans has always been measured in courage and confidence. The Republicans believe the wagon train will not make it to the frontier unless some of our old, some of our young, and some of our weak are left behind by the side of the trail. The strong will inherit the land!"

-1984

■ ■ ■

"...President Reagan told us from the beginning that he believed in a kind of Social Darwinism - survival of the fittest. Government can't do everything we were told. So it should settle for taking care of the strong and hope that economic ambition and chairity will do the rest. Make the rich richer and what falls from their table will be enough for the middle class and those trying to make it into the middle class."

-1984

■ ■ ■

We must get the American public to look past the glitter, beyond the showmanship...to reality, to the hard substance of things. And we will do that not so much with speeches that sound good as with speeches that are good and sound. Not so much with speeches that bring people to their feet as with speeches that bring people to their senses."

■ ■ ■   -1984

CRIME AND PUNISHMENT

When President Bush nominated Clarence Thomas to become a Supreme Court justice, Governor Cuomo joined a chorus of critics who questioned the decision.

"As a lawyer and judge, the record indicates he is not stellar...His instinct is apparently to diminish the importance of individual rights, individual freedoms."

-1991

■ ■ ■

During an appearance on *Face the Nation* in the summer of 1991, the governor cast further doubts on the selection of Thomas to the nation's highest court.

"It's difficult for me to believe that the President was informed by his counsels that Clarence Thomas was the very best lawyer judge available. I don't believe that for a minute. Well, if that wasn't the truth...then what credentials did he have? I think that the suspicion his race might have been deemed relevant is a plausible suspicion."

-1991

■ ■ ■

"...Clarence Thomas, in terms of personal achievement, is an extraordinary human being as far as I could tell...(But) that I could probably easily name 10 other blacks, if you're interested in an African-American who had better credentials as lawyers and as judges... And that's the way the thing ought to be decided - him as a judge, him as a lawyer - his ability to write, his experience. If you get into political ideology, then I don't like his political ideology at all..."

-1991

■ ■ ■

"Political ideology ought not to be part of selecting a Supreme Court justice. For 200 years all presidents have made it part of selecting Supreme Court justices. But when you start announcing political positions in advance as the Republicans do when they select a Conservative, then you make political ideology a part of the discussion before the Senate. And I think that's going to happen."

-1991

■ ■ ■

At the height of the deficit crisis in early 1990, Cuomo proposed delaying constuction of four prisons to save the state $80 million. But he warned state lawmakers they would have to accept his proposals for alternatives to prison sentences if the halt in construction was to be realistic.

"Would that I could say the crime rate has slowed down so much we don't need the prisons. You'll have to change some laws, change some practices, in order to slow down the need for cells."

-1991

■ ■ ■

When a caller phoned the governor's statewide radio show to discuss a furor over the continuation of an experiment which allowed television cameras and tape recorders in the courts, the caller suggested that such media coverage encourages lawyers to become actors before the court. Cuomo, an attorney himself, had an interesting observation.

"Now wait a minute. If you have a jury trial, aren't lawyers already actors?"

-1991

■ ■ ■

When violence broke out on the St. Regis Indian Reservation, the governor dispatched state troopers to try to restore peace to a community that was bitterly divided in a dispute over gambling. Cuomo stressed repeatedly his desire to help negotiate a peaceful settlement. He said an early step would be the establishment of a Mohawk police force on the reservation.

"The tragedies of the recent past underscore the wisdom of encouraging this approach... Such an arrangement could provide a reliable police force controlled by the residents of the reservation, sufficient to maintain an ordered community with an appropriate degree of self governance."

-1990

■ ■ ■

"For the last five days and nights, there have been no reports of violence or major disorders on the St. Regis Akwesasne Reservation. I call upon all elements of the community to keep this attitude of reason and calm as they attempt to work out the difficulties that currently divide them."

-1990

■ ■ ■

As one of the governor's statewide radio call-in shows was winding down, Cuomo tried to provide some levity as a Brooklyn man named Seymour came on the line.

"Seymour, you ever hear of Olsen and Johnson - *Hellzapoppin?*"

"The Health Department?" the confused caller asked.

"No! *Hellzapoppin,*" Cuomo responded with a hardy laugh. But he quickly realized that Seymour was not on the line to crack jokes or to provide levity for thousands of listeners across the state. Seymour was frightened. Terrified of the growing crime scourge.

"You're no longer the governor of the sovereign state. You've lost sovereignty to the drug lords...They are killing people on the street here. You can't go out. Bring in the National Guard."

"Let's remember history a little bit, Seymour. It's not a good precedent to bring in a military presence...I proposed that we raise a new tax for more police. Mayor Dinkins agrees. That's what we need...You're in Flatbush? Near what?...Ocean Avenue. I know the area. Take care, now."

-1990

■ ■ ■

At a conference of chief justices in Lake George, New York, the governor chastised the federal courts for giving increasing authority to state courts. Cuomo expressed belief that passing along more power to the state courts has led to uneven and unequal treatment of cases from state-to-state.

"Our national values, national resolve and national capacity are strengthened when we have a firm set of *overarching* standards that apply to every American, no matter where he or she lives. I do not believe that the fundamental liberties and rights of members of our national community should vary, depending on what side of the state line one happens to be on at the moment.

-1990

■ ■ ■

Cuomo once vetoed a bill that would have boosted the penalty for possessing a loaded machine gun during commission of a drug-related crime. The governor assailed the legislation as a "flawed and feeble" substitution to his proposed ban on all assault weapons. This, despite supporters insistence that the law should have afforded prosecutors yet another tool for cracking down on drug-related activities.

But Cuomo argued the existing law already penalized such criminals and he said machine guns are relatively uncommon.

"Today, an assault weapon is 20 times more likely to be used in a crime than a conventional weapon and certainly even more likely to be used in a crime than a machine gun."

-1989

■ ■ ■

Widespread concern that the drug epidemic was forcing police officers to grapple with increasing violence, a new law was unveiled that aimed to improve support, education and other benefits for the families of law enforcers who were slain in the line of duty. Cuomo's proposal underscored his earlier assertions that the state would have to provide more money and other resources for police. He said law enforcers are confronting more dangers than ever before.

"It has never been what it is now. There's never been the weapons, there's never been the madness, there's never been the crack…The uniqueness of the moment calls for unique responses."

-1989

■ ■ ■

Even during excruciating fiscal times, Cuomo urged decision-makers in Albany to beef up drug treatment programs. He labelled the drug crisis "the single most ominous phenomenon of our times, our greatest vulnerability now and the most severe threat to our future."

-1989

■ ■ ■

Warning that New York State was facing a staggering increase in it's prison population in the coming years, Governor Cuomo called on lawmakers to support plans for countering prison overcrowding. Among the strategies he advanced were new programs for treating sex offenders, initiatives for helping DWI-offenders stay away from alcohol after their release and more elaborate parole and probation programs.

"We cannot keep building prisons forever. The taxpayers can't afford it, and we know that imprisonment is not always the best and most appropriate form of correction."

-1988

■ ■ ■

During a graduation ceremony for more than 250 state troppers, the governor told the force that members must protect the virtues of a civilized society by living model lives.

"Your oath and uniform give you responsibilities most people prefer not to have, a responsibility for an entire society...for living not only by the law, but for the law."

-1987

■ ■ ■

During a speech to members of the National Association for the Advancement of Colored People, Cuomo said judges should approach issues with open minds.

"It is wrong in my opinion for a judge to go on the Supreme

Court...bench with his mind made up on abortion or any issues. If it becomes clear that he has already made up his mind, then he should not be on the bench. Can you call a strike before the pitch is thrown? How can you make a decision before reading the evidence?"

-1987

■ ■ ■

"There is less respect for the law in this country than ever before.... Stand at a street corner late at night and see how many people disregard red lights – just drive through them as if they weren't there. Look at the numbers of people who, despite all the warnings and pleadings and threats, continue to drive while drunk and to kill other human beings in the process. Consider that some communities have begun walling themselves off from the outside world, as the villages and towns of Western Europe did at the outset of the Dark Ages.... Sometimes all of us become impatient with the law and **feel** it stands in the way of real justice. But remember – that's God's judgment to make. We lesser beings must live by the laws of our human society."

-1985

■ ■ ■

Even before he officially took the oath of office, Cuomo spent much time talking about criminal justice. During an interview published by the *Los Angeles Times*, Cuomo lamented the fact that crime was a dominant topic in his first election bid.

"I was unhappy to have to talk so much about criminal justice. It is a shame we have to spend so much time just protecting ourselves from injury, but we do. It is a bad time in the streets, very bad. You have to deal with balancing the budget... but you have to at the same time, find a way to do something about the criminal justice system that's terribly inefficient."

-1982

■ ■ ■

Cuomo sat down to watch a television news report about the gubernatorial slug fest between himself and Republican candidate Lew Lehrman. When Lehrman was shown on the tube talking about "thuggery," Cuomo quipped:

"You accuse a ciminal of thuggery and he'll think you're complimenting him!"

-1982

■■■

The governor once coined a colorful phrase to describe muggers who plague New York City. He described them as the "midnight mayors of the metropolis." Cuomo's daughter, Maria, was mugged twice.

-1982

■■■

In a speech to the Mid Atlantic States Correction Association, Cuomo noted that there have always been law breakers.

"Adam and Eve conspired to bite the apple and Cain slew Abel; jewels were stolen from Egyptian tombs, and acts of murder, even genocide have been performed down through the ages. The penchant for evil and violence is forever present in man. But it does vary from time to time in the intensity of its impression in our society. And today, it is particularly intense.

-1991

■■■

The Cuomo family has experienced first-hand the feelings of pain and outrage that come from being victimized by criminals. When Cuomo was Lieutenant Governor, his 18-year-old daughter was mugged twice by the same assailant in the middle of the afternoon. It occurred just down the street from the family's home.

"Now, she'll never be the same unless God is very, very good to us. And we're on our knees thanking God that she wasn't badly hurt; that she wasn't raped, that nothing worse happened to her - that she didn't get killed. So I feel it - we feel it - the passion. If my son ever gets his hands on this guy - forget my son - if I ever did, I cannot predict how I would behave. I'm not a saint and I'm not God. And if you stood that person in front of me and said 'there he is,' I don't know what I would do."

-1982

■ ■ ■

"The thing that is most obvious is that criminal justice is an enormous problem, much too large for an electric chair, a tough new gun law or even an army of relentlessly hard judges. Achieving it will take money and agreements, it will take publicity and discussion, it will require sacrifice and may even cost some careers. But we - you and I - must do what we can because the safety of the people is government's primary obligation. We have failed in that obligation for far too long.

-1982

■ ■ ■

THE DEATH PENALTY DEBATE

Few of Cuomo's stands have generated more controversy than his steadfast oppostion to the death penalty. The governor has repeatedly blocked Legislature efforts to restore capital punishment, vetoing the measure very year since he took office in 1983.

"The death penalty legitimizes the ultimate act of vengeance in the name of the state, violates fundamental human rights, fuels a mistaken belief by some that justice is being served and demeans those who strive to preserve human life and dignity."

-1991

■ ■ ■

Cuomo has been a staunch advocate of an alternative to capital punishment; he calls it "death by incarceration." The governor proposed eliminating any possibility of parole. As for allowing pardons or clemency, Cuomo said:

"(To) eliminate any doubt on this point... we should amend our

State Constitution to specifically deny commutations of sentences of life without parole."

-1991

■ ■ ■

The governor's tough stand against the death penalty has been a perennial hot potato on his statewide radio call-in show. During his *"Ask the Governor"* program, Cuomo argued capital punishment has historically been unevenly applied.

"I don't remember the last time a person with a bank account was ever sentenced to the electric chair, unless he or she was a mad person and volunteered to do it. Almost always if you have the wealth, you can buy your way out of these situations, let's be candid. You get yourself a good lawyer, you don't go to the electric chair."

-1990

■ ■ ■

"They (state lawmakers) want death. It sounds tough, but it's not strength; it's the ultimate surrender... All the emphasis is on symbolism... not on substance."

-1990

■ ■ ■

"The death penalty is debasing. If we were to bring it back, it would return us to the company of South Africa, the Soviet Union, Iran, Saudi Arabia and others – none of the nations we normally point to as our peers in civilization... A very important part of the argument of the death penalty has been that the people manifestly want it... For six years, I have been saying I don't believe people want it, and if legislators were really honest about it, they would put two propositions on the ballot – the death penalty, and life imprisonment without parole, no possibility of clemency. And life imprisonment without parole would win."

-1989

■ ■ ■

"(There) is no evidence the death penalty is a deterrent to crime. Violent crime has not uniformly decreased in states that have enacted capital punishment, nor has it increased in states that have abolished capital punishment."

–1982

"The real deterrent to crime is found not in draconian punishment or circumventing due process, but in the certainty of swift, sure justice. Determinate sentencing is a major element in restoring that certainty to (the) criminal justice system."

–1985

"Instead of talking about the real issues of crime and the conditions that breed it, the public has been mesmerized by the electric chair. Mesmerized. But the answer to crime isn't vengeance – it's more police, more judges, a better prosecutorial system, determinate sentencing, and more jail cells."

–1982

Even before he became governor, the state's number two man was espousing his vehement opposition to the death penalty. He addressed the issue during a police conference.

"The truth is, I don't believe it works... I don't believe it deters (or) protects my daughter or my mother. I believe it is a cop out and I believe that politicians have used it for years to keep from answering the real questions like: 'how come we're short some 100,000 police? How come the state troopers are paid so little in this state when they're supposed to be so important? How come we have run out of prison cells? How come probation and parole are not all they should be? How did we get there?' Politicians don't want to deal with these questions. So they deal with a simple question – the electric chair – and that gets everybody off the hook."

–1982

MEDIA SPARRING MATCHES

When state leaders were grappling with a deficit crisis in the spring of 1991, Cuomo became even more accessible to reporters. It was not unusual to hear the governor doing live phone interviews on radio stations across the state, using such forums to point an accusing finger at the Legislature for its role in fueling a precedent-setting budget stalemate.

Cuomo opened his office doors to Buffalo reporter Brian Meyer, managing editor of news at WBEN Radio. While fiscal issues dominated the candid 20-minute chat, the governor's clever handling of questions dealing with his political future exemplified his ability to deflect attention from certain topics. Put simply, Cuomo sometimes enjoys playing with the press.

Meyer: "You spoke at a graduation ceremony in Rhode Island over the weekend, once again fueling speculation that you might be eyeing a run for the White House..."

Cuomo: "How did I do that?"

Meyer: "Well, whenever you go out of state and speak, those media mavens say 'ah ha? The governor is thinking of running for president.' I've got to ask you; I've asked you dozens of times in Buffalo --"

Cuomo: "Wait a minute, Brian. Just a minute. I am now speaking in Albany. Why does the subject come up now?"

Meyer: (Pause) "You and Mayor Griffin should get together, because you guys are masters at turning the tables on reporters.

Cuomo: "Mayor Griffin is a master at turning the tables?"

Meyer: "You know what I've told the mayor? When I become an elected official, then I'll answer the questions."

Cuomo: "You know what I say on behalf of Mayor Griffin? You're lucky he turns the table and doesn't throw it at you, instead!"

Meyer: "But governor, what about the other topic?"

Cuomo: "Okay, let me give you a good clear answer. I think he *shouldn't* throw the table at you!"

-1991

∎∎∎

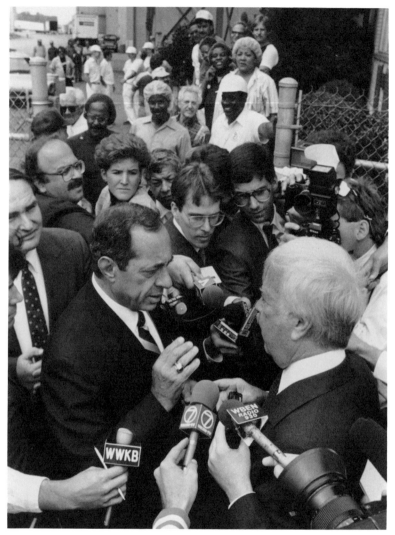

Joe Traver for The New York Times

The governor labelled his Republican sparring partner "Pop-Up Pierre." During the 1990 gubernatorial campaign, Pierre Rinfret was prone to showing up at Cuomo news events unannounced. Such a confrontation occurred outside the General Mills cereal plant in downtown Buffalo. Reporters and grain workers watch as the two political foes trade barbs outside the plant.

Several years earlier, there was also speculation that Cuomo was secretly angling for the Democratic presidential nod. This, despite repeated assertions by the governor that he was not running. At one point, he blasted the media for refusing to print the truth.

"I wish somebody, sometime would write a piece that says 'let's face it, he was telling the truth. Nobody has... You've done everything but call me a liar. You said that I was cute. You said that I misplayed the game. You said that I was really waiting for another scenario... It really comes down to my credibility or yours... All through my career I have made promises and lived up to them. I told you in '84 (I wasn't running), I told you in '86, I told you in '87. And you guys then do columns that say 'What did he really intend? Did he have a mafia background? Did he have skeletons in his closet? Did his son get involved? Did he think he couldn't win? Why don't you just write the truth?"

–1988

Several years earlier, there was also speculation that Cuomo was

The governor became somewhat of a Jimmy Olsen in the summer of 1988. He became a newspaper reporter for a day, following a challenge by a staffer at the *Jamestown Post Journal* who suggested that Cuomo try the business before he knocked it.

"I saw this as an opportunity to encourage people to think about getting to know one another's operations.

"I don't think, ugh, I'm not sure that print would be my, ugh, my strength, ugh, I don't think reporting would be. I think reporting is too hard."

–1988

During a speech to the New York City Press Club, the governor expressed belief that reporters must be more careful now than ever before about what they write and broadcast about people. He said the increased incidence of libel cases could ultimately threaten freedom of the press.

"We are approaching a time when shifts in our law may seriously dilute the protection of the press and thereby weaken the fabric of this society. (A press) regarded by the public as reckless invites the attention of the Supreme Court and attempts to perform corrective judicial surgery."

-1982

■ ■ ■

"If you want to be protected against the regulation that I think would be an impediment to the free flow of information, you had better regulate yourselves, and what that means, if I may say so to the press, is don't be so thin-skinned. If every once in a while a politician goes crazy and says 'I think you're imperfect,' I don't think the media should suddenly get up-in-arms and take this as a challenge to the First Amendment. Rather, what they should do is say 'I wonder if that story was inacurrate, I wonder if I could do it better?'"

-1986

■ ■ ■

Over the years, the governor has become a verbal sparring partner with members of the Fourth Estata. One such lively exchange occurred in the waning months of his first term when he engaged in what he described as a "Socratic dialogue" on the subject of organized crime.

"You're telling me that mafia is an organization, and I'm telling you it's a lot of baloney."

-1986

■ ■ ■

But Cuomo hasn't always been prone to ascribe such importance to the power of the printed word. In the same year that he made the above statement, suggesting the media makes reality, he casually dismissed a *New York Times* account of a recent gubernatorial debate.

"This is just a walnut in the batter of eternity. It plops down on

the surface, makes a brief impression, and then disappears...
Tomorrow, no one will remember."

-1982

Still, only two months earlier, Cuomo was discussing the influence
that the press wields in lofty terms. When the *New York Times*
published a front page story that indicated Edward Koch had the
convention locked up, Cuomo commented:

"Given its power, this paper can kill you."

-1982

"We delivered and then they weaseled. They said 'Well, we know we said that, but...' You cannot do business that way. You couldn't do it in my father's grocery store and you can't do it in Western New York."

– 1990

The target of Cuomo's wrath was the Erie County Legislature. The issue: a fiscal crisis that caused a two-day shutdown of the region's public transit system; a shutdown that made national headlines.

The governor lambasted lawmakers for backing out of a deal to provide the transportation authority with a financial bail-out plan.

"Find a revenue stream as you promised... or else explain to your people how you could come to Albany, make a deal, then back away from it and expect us to do anything for you in the future."

– 1990

At one point in this transit system tug-of-war, the governor even issued a threat to Erie County leaders, suggesting that they could have a tough time securing state aid in the future if they failed to rescue the fiscally-malnourished bus and rail systems.

"It costs you all your other requests; you're risking your credibility... If you go back on your word with no other explanation other than opportunism, you're going to be in bad trouble."

(County leaders eventually approved a bail-out package for the Niagara Frontier Transportation Authority, but only after the bus and rail systems were shut down for two days. The controversial package included a new tax on local real estate sales.)

– 1990

Erie County Executive Dennis Gorski is known for delivering lengthy introductions whenever he is assigned the task of bringing a prominent speaker to the microphone. He gave a particularly wordy introduction when Governor Cuomo appeared at the Buffalo Convention Center in 1990 for a get-out-the-vote rally. Cuomo sauntered to the podium, paused, and said:

"Every time (Gorski) gives me a long introduction, it costs me a fortune in Albany."

– 1990

■ ■ ■

Joe Traver/Bison Baseball

When Western New Yorkers celebrated opening day at Pilot Field in 1988, Governor Cuomo was on hand for the festivities. The state was instrumental in helping to finance the new baseball stadium in downtown Buffalo. Standing to the right of Cuomo are Robert Rich Jr. and his wife, Mindy, owners of the Buffalo Bisons.

■ ■ ■

When talk turned to expanding Pilot Field, Buffalo's nationally-acclaimed minor league baseball stadium, Cuomo promised to help in the effort.

"We'll be helpful. Count on it... Obviously, if I'm going to be there advocating, I'm going to have to put some state money where my rhetoric is. The exact way in which we'll participate is something I'm working on."

– 1990

■ ■ ■

Still, the governor made it clear that Western New York leaders would have to be realistic in the requests they submit to the state for assistance in upgrading the downtown arena in which the Buffalo Sabres play and to improve Rich Stadium, home of the Buffalo Bills.

"I'm not going to con you. You can't have everything you keep asking for. The Knox family (owners of the Buffalo Sabres) can ask... and we'll build them a building and build you a larger stadium and give you the World Games... But you're not going to get it all."

– 1990

■ ■ ■

Cuomo frequently talked about Buffalo's sports teams during his visits to the Niagara Frontier. He rooted for them, and ribbed them depending on the teams' performance. At one point during a briefing on his Liberty Scholarship program, the governor gave some advice to the Buffalo Bills.

"Get an offense, will ya?!"

Three months later, the Bills would make their Super Bowl debut.

– 1990

■ ■ ■

The governor's relationship with Jimmy Griffin, Buffalo's unpredictable mayor, has been a topsy-turvy one at best. Back in 1980, Griffin was showering Lieutenant Governor Cuomo with praise for his role in leading a task force aimed at bringing Western New York back from the brink of financial doom.

"If I'm in a fight and I want someone to be on my side, it will be the lieutenant governor," Mayor Griffin told a gathering at the former Statler Hotel. "We need Mario Cuomo in state government, or any other government he'd like to try."

But the relationship soured in the mid 1980s, when the mayor blamed Cuomo for many of the ills that faced localities. Griffin once even eyed a possible run against Cuomo. At one point, hizzoner questioned Cuomo's judgment on an issue, suggesting that he must have been "hit in the head with a pitched ball" during his brief career in major league baseball.

But Cuomo regularly wears a reminder of his more friendly days with Griffin. He has a gold Seiko watch that adorns his wrist.

"This watch was given to me in 1980 by Jimmy Giffin… He denies it now."

– 1990

Joe Traver/Courier Express

Although Buffalo Mayor Jimmy Griffin (left) has been prone to telling Cuomo to "mind his own business" and has hurled other insults at the governor, the two leaders manage to keep a civil front when Cuomo visits the Niagara Frontier.

■ ■ ■

"I did show (the watch) to the mayor once a few years back. 'Jimmy, don't you remember this?'"

– 1990

■ ■ ■

The Seiko watch wasn't the only gift he received from Buffalo's feisty chief executive. The mayor once gave him a black, size 36 Louisville slugger; the baseball bat was a sign of Griffin's admiration for Cuomo. But when the lieutenant governor called on Griffin to endorse him in his primary battle against New York City Mayor Ed Koch, Griffin refused.

Cuomo reflected on Griffin's change of heart, holding his baseball bat. He asked his 12-year-old son, Christopher for some political advice. How should he approach his one-time friend, Jimmy Griffin, and try to convince him to support his candidacy.

Christopher thought about the dilemma for a moment, then came up with the answer.

"Hit him on the head with the bat," the boy suggested.

– 1982

■ ■ ■

Governor Cuomo would occasionally take sides in Buffalo-based political duels. He backed his long-time Albany ally Dennis Gorski in his 1987 fight to topple Republican incumbent Ed Rutkowski. During a spirited rally in Erie County, Cuomo told the cheering crowd:

"I'm here because I want to be as close as I can get to the next county executive. It's very important to me in Albany that I stay close to the important people and Gorski is surely going to be one of the important people in this state after election day."

– 1987

■ ■ ■

Cuomo attacked incumbent Ed Rutkowski, noting that his administration was at the helm when the county faced a devastating deficit crisis that nearly destroyed the county's financial future.

"You wouldn't play a football game without a playbook, and we've got a county executive who wants to manage the place from his recollection."

(Rutkowski was a former Buffalo Bill.)

– 1987

■ ■ ■

Speaking of Erie County's deficit crisis, the governor dealt with the issue during a television appearance in the mid 1980s. He defended the state from claims that it could have done more to help the county out of the deficit doldrums, using a story to make his point. In this anecdote, he likened Rutkowski to an elderly apple vendor.

"Every day, this man passes by an old lady dressed in ragged clothes selling apples, and every day he puts in a quarter but doesn't take an apple. Then, one day, the woman stops him and says she has to tell him something. 'I know,' the man answers. 'You want to know why I never take an apple.' 'No,' the woman says. 'I just want to tell you that the price is now 50 cents.'"

– 1985

■ ■ ■

But even Cuomo's political allies were not immune to the governor's occasional barbs. When County Executive Gorski publicly urged the state to rethink plans to continue reducing income taxes, the governor told a radio reporter in Buffalo:

"That's interesting, (and) if Dennis were governor it would be relevant."

– 1988

■ ■ ■

On many occasions, Cuomo's visits to Western New York centered on his administration's efforts to improve the local economy. He once met with officials at the Ford Motor Co. Stamping Plant in a Buffalo suburb where he handed over funds to train production workers to deal with new equipment.

"It shows, for example, that you don't have to give up on manufacturing, you don't have to give up in this global competition. You are as good as they are, even better... If you do the training you should do. If you produce the type of quality you're capable of (producing)."

– 1989

... ON THE BIG APPLE

Cuomo is prone to singing songs of praise for his hometown. When a caller mentioned New York City on the governor's monthly radio show, Cuomo rallied to its defense.

"There's more good than bad in this great city; there's just no question about that. That's why I've been here all my life and that's why I'm sure I'll die here. Not right away, though, I hope!"

– 1991

■■■

"People upstate have been taught by their politicians to believe that New York City is a great drain on the state. The truth is, New York City contributes a lot more than it takes from the state. It gives more than it gets per capita."

– 1991

■■■

During the budget debacle in 1991, Cuomo occasionally found himself at odds with some of the policies of New York City Mayor David Dinkins. One flap stemmed from the city's approval of contracts that awarded its major unions raises of 5 percent. In contrast, Cuomo proposed a wage freeze for the state workforce. He seemed to scold New York City leaders for their stand on pay hikes.

"I'm not taking the position that you have no right to do salary increases ... That's your business. I'm telling you when you do the salary increases, as you did – and I congratulate you on your courage – then you come up here and say you're in trouble because you didn't get $600 million from us, when you spend $1 billion on salary increases, I regard there to be a disconnect logic to that."

– 1991

■■■

Speaking to the New York City Bar Association in 1989, Cuomo told lawyers that crime in the city has changed life dramatically.

"The wealthy and the business community are guarded by the largest army of unofficial security agents in the history of the nation. Parks and other public places are declared off-limits to the prudent, and surrendered to marauders. (The situation is so bad) that large numbers of our people throw their fists in the air and shout for 'death' (capital punishment) as a solution ..."

– 1989

■ ■ ■

Governor Cuomo urged state lawmakers to pass laws that would force New York City police officers and firefighters to live within city boundaries.

"(It would) create a whole new sensitivity, because everybody on the ... force would be somebody who lives in the town that he's trying to protect."

– 1988

■ ■ ■

... ON CIVIL RIGHTS

When Cuomo signed a bill to hike penalties for harming a guide dog for the disabled, he used the event to blast Senate Republicans for allegedly refusing to give minorities and gays similar protection.

"The Senate majority's position ... appears to be that it is willing to protect a special class of animals through this bill, but is unwilling to protect gay people, the disabled, blacks or any of the other protected classes of persons against the international acts of a criminal ... The Senate majority has stated that it opposes in principle any law that provides special sanctions for crimes against a special class of victims. Nonetheless, the Senate approved this bill, which correctly makes it a special crime to harm a special group of victims – animals that assist persons with a disability."

– 1989

■ ■ ■

In a speech to the state's Black and Puerto Rican Legislative Caucus, the governor challenged the Legislature to adopt laws that would impose stiffer penalties against perpetrators of racial violence.

"Assault and murder and all these terrible crimes are evil enough. But if you do it because he's a nigger, because he's a spic, because he's a dago, because he's a Catholic, because he's a gay, then we have to punish you even more severly. Because that's an insidious evil that needs special punishment."

– 1988

Joe Traver for The New York Times

The governor leads youngsters in a rousing but off-key rendition of Happy Birthday *in honor of grade-schooler Tony Goalstein. Cuomo was hosting a state budget forum at the Buffalo Waterfront School in 1986.*

...ON EDUCATION

When the Bush administration argued that channeling more money into the nation's education system would not necessarily improve the schools, Cuomo challenged the president's position.

"Why didn't they ever say that about defense? When they get to education, they say 'No, with education, you can do it with management.' Why couldn't you do it in defense with management? You need money for missiles, but not money for schoolhouses. You need money for generals, but not money for our teachers. I don't understand how, when it's convenient, you can say 'You can't throw money at a problem, but if it's defense, you have to throw money at it.'"

– 1991

■ ■ ■

The governor frequently used his statewide radio call-in talk show to defend his administration's commitment to education.

"(Even after budget cuts), we still have the most generous state program in the United States of America, with more tuition assistance and more scholarships, and lower tuition than most of the schools in our own region."

One caller asked the governor why he vetoed $500 million in additional school aid.

"Because it was Monopoly money. It was phony money. You would have never seen it anyway. The budget was unbalanced.."

When the caller persisted, saying she would have rather seen the budget cuts hit the prisons than the classrooms, Cuomo became somewhat testy.

"You would have to close the prisons and put the killers on the streets. Is that what you want?"

When the same caller suggested there are too many frills offered to prisoners, Cuomo had an immediate response.

"If you took away all their postage stamps, if you took away all the television sets and locked (prisoners) in their rooms and fed them one meal a day; if you cut the number of prison guards in half, you still wouldn't have enough money to do the $500 million that you want for education."

But the caller was persistent. Robin kept pressing the governor about the state's overall commitment to funding education. Finally, Cuomo said in a resigned tone:

"I have the feeling I can never win with you, Robin. It's like talking to Matilda (Cuomo's wife.) I'm never gonna win. I can tell."

At this point, the radio interviewer chimed in: "I hope Matilda heard that!"

The governor ignored the comment, focusing his attention on the skeptical caller.

"Robin," Cuomo said, "I'm not asking you to vote for me. Just feel sorry for me."

– 1991

■ ■ ■

When leaders in the state university system proposed to hike tuition if Cuomo and the Legislature failed to appropriate more funding in the 1989-90 state budget, the governor attacked the position.

"It's an outrage. It's wrong. (If they can't save money in other ways), then they should get new managers. You can't save a penny? There's no automobile you can't get rid of? There are no prices you can bring down? No corners you can cut? You run an absolutely flawlessy efficient business operation? Who are you, some genius?"

– 1989

■ ■ ■

During an earlier radio interview, Cuomo bristled at the notion that his proposed budget cuts are cruel to education programs and other youth-related programs.

"If you're saying we need more money for children, I agree with you. We need more money for pre-K, for community schools, for smaller classes and longer school years. But we cannot afford it now ... A lot of people are saying raise taxes and spend the money on children. If you raise taxes in the city of New York higher than they are now, I'm telling you, you will drive out so much business, you will be jeopardizing the jobs that you are trying to teach your children to be able to handle. It's like cutting off your nose to spite your face."

– 1991

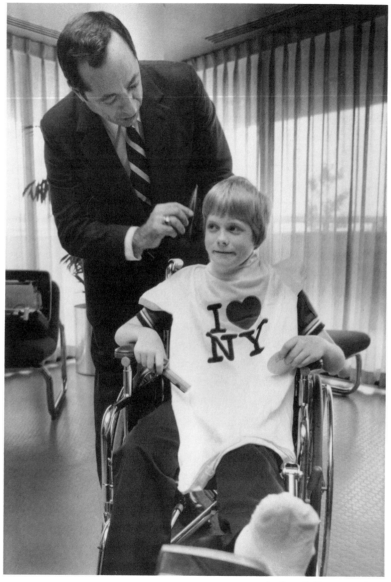

Joe Traver for The New York Times

Decade of the Child. *Governor Cuomo has stressed the state's responsibility for financing programs that help children and families. His critics have accused him of being more talk than action.*

■■■

Many of the governor's annual State of the State messages have focused on the needs of society's young.

"The children entering our kindergartens and junior high schools today will be the work force and taxpayers of tomorrow, the backbone of our economy in the new century ... We must make wise investments now in our children."

– 1988

■■■

... ON THE ENVIRONMENT

When state officials took steps to try to reopen West Valley, a rural community not far from Buffalo, to more low-level nuclear waste, many residents and elected leaders waged an aggressive fight against the plan. The state offered a generous financial incentive package to the region to accept the radioactive material.

Cuomo confronted throngs of infuriated West Valley residents when he visited Buffalo in the summer of 1991. As he stepped out of his car, a sign-toting demonstrator pointed to a little girl, who approached the governor and showed him a rusty screw.

"She has a gift for you, governor," the protestor said.

Cuomo cringed.

"Oh, I hate to think of what the symbolism of the screw is."

"Well, that's what we think happened to West Valley."

The governor handed back the screw. "Thank you, dear," he said to the child.

"But she doesn't need it," the protester told Cuomo.

"You could have (delivered your message) a little more elegantly, especially if you used a child," the visibly-irritated governor said.

– 1991

■■■

When protestors pointed out local residents rejected the nuclear waste plan in a non-binding referendum, Cuomo dismissed the results.

"What if we started taking referenda statewide. Do you really want to live that way? You want to look up at your television screen at 6 O'clock and it says 'Today, it's says no death penalty or no welfare for poor people.' You really want to live by referenda? I wouldn't."

– 1991

■ ■ ■

Later in the day, a reporter asked Cuomo about allegations that his administration was involved in secret, behind-the-scenes negotiations regarding the fate of West Valley.

Meyer: "What about residents' claims that there has been secret deal-making?"

Cuomo: "Was there a secret deal made?"

Meyer: "When I become governor, I'll start answering questions."

Cuomo: "Do *you* know if there was one?"

Meyer: "No, but residents feel there was."

Cuomo: "Well, neither of us know. Maybe it was *really* secret, right?"

Meyer: "Governor, were you part of any back-room deals?"

Cuomo: "Oh, look at the (television) camera and say that!"

Meyer: "Were you?"

Cuomo: "No! Not front room, back room, middle room, upstairs, downstairs. I didn't do it in the middle of a field. I didn't even know it was being done. With the legislature, we get accused of that. But I didn't make any back room deals."

– 1991

■ ■ ■

... ON ETHNICITY

The governor takes great pride in his Italian heritage. In discussing the issue, he once acknowledged that many Italian-Americans, himself included, have been victimized by unfair stereotypes at some point in their lives, but he said he did not think his heritage has been a professional drawback.

"Personally, I don't believe it has ever been a substantial

impediment in my own life, as annoying and irritating as it has been. If anything, my ethnicity, my origins as an Italian-American, have probably helped me a good deal more than they have hurt me."

– 1987

■ ■ ■

"In 1982, when (New York City) Mayor Ed Koch was ahead of me by 38 percentage points, people said I couldn't win (as governor) because I would never get the Jewish vote. I won the governor's race over Koch, who up till then was the most popular politician in the state. So I reject this line that an Italian can't be president. Ethnicity is part of our strength. Americans relish it ... I say it's a lot of baloney that this country is still so crude that people won't vote for a jew, an Italian, a black person.

– 1987

■ ■ ■

Cuomo's ethnicity was raised in the media on more than one occasion. When the governor read in a newspaper column a passage that suggested an Italian couldn't be elected president, he told a reporter:

"If anything could make me change my mind about running for the presidency, it's people talking about 'An Italian Catholic can't do it, a Catholic can't do it.'"

– 1986

■ ■ ■

"Look, we're Italian, we're very proud of it ... Wouldn't it be great if those of us who remember being called guineas and wops and dagos will now stop talking about people as spics and niggers? Wouldn't it be terrible if we did to the people that came after us what we think some people did to us?"

– 1986

■ ■ ■

When Mario Cuomo was first elected governor in the fall of 1982, he was acutely aware of the fact that New York had elected its first-ever Italian-American (In fact, lieutenant Governor Alfred DeBello was also Italian.) Said Cuomo:

"After 200 years, New York finally did it right."

– 1982

∎∎∎

... ON FEDERAL GOVERNMENT FLAPS

Few Democrats have been more articulate or more outspoken than Cuomo when it involves the administrations of Republicans George Bush and Ronald Reagan. The governor's unrelenting attacks on GOP philosophies, particularly domestic policies, have frequently served as the fuel for speculation that Cuomo might have his sights on the White House.

When the nation went to war against Saddam Hussein, Cuomo charged the Bush administration with turning its back on pressing economic problems at home.

"I don't see (Bush) sending the same kind of energy into the economic struggle as he's sending over to the sands of Arabia ... The economic threat to this nation is at least as great as the threat from Saddam Hussein, and everybody who is responsible knows it. It appears from here that (Bush) prefers to deal with the international geopolitics rather than the streets of our cities ... that he prefers to deal with the foreign policy questions instead of the domestic economic problems that have driven the people into anger over taxes and spending."

– 1991

∎∎∎

"Here we are flailing, confused, no leadership, No clear path to economic strength. A federal government that has copped out entirely."

– 1991

■ ■ ■

"85 percent of the American people are living in states where the taxes are going up, the services are going down. And Washington has declared that there is no economic problem and that we have a budget we can't touch for four or five years."

– 1991

■ ■ ■

During a speech to reporters attending a National Press Club function in the nation's capitol, Governor Cuomo assailed a federal proposal to eliminate the deductibility of state and local taxes.

"We've already been told that the critics of this plan are 'sharks getting ready to bite.' And it's true. Perhaps the sharks are gathering. But that's because there's blood in the water – *our* blood. The blood of the states and localities being told that there's no room in the federal lifeboat, that if some are to prosper, the rest of us will have to be thrown overboard.

– 1985

■ ■ ■

... ON FITNESS

The headlines read: *Cuomo doubles as fitness model.* The governor once agreed to pose for photos with hunky Hollywood mega-star Arnold Schwarzenegger. It was all part of the body-builder's push to enlist the support of governors for better physical fitness training for children. Schwarzenegger chaired the President's Council on Physical Fitness. He had starred in the hit flick *Twins* with Danny DeVito.

As Schwarzenegger posed for photographs with New York's governor, he quipped: "This is not *Twins II.*"

As for Cuomo's physical condition, Schwarzenegger took a good look at the governor and said: "I know he's in good shape."

But the body-builder made it clear he was not referring to the Democratic governor's political ideologies.

– 1991

■ ■ ■

... ON FREE ENTERPRISE

In a 1985 lecture at Yale University, Cuomo talked about the free enterprise system that has been the foundation for progress in America.

"We believe, therefore, that government must accommodate the producers of wealth; indeed, that it must encourage as many people as possible to pursue the honest rewards of imagination, ambition and hard work. But we recognize that, even at its best, the free enterprise system won't be able to include everyone, that there'll always be those left out; the frail, the poor, the old, those without skills or hope, sometimes without even a roof over their heads. We are confident that government can act progressively and pragmatically to help care for those who simply can't care for themselves."

– 1985

■ ■ ■

... ON GASOLINE PRICES

The governor took a lot of heat for proposing to boost the state's tax on gasoline as a strategy for raising revenues. But in an Albany interview with Buffalo reporter Brian Meyer, Cuomo defended his controversial plan.

"What are you gonna do for your roads and bridges? Do you want an income tax? That's what the Speaker wants. He wants a $600 million income tax that would tax people making $11,000 a year, whether they have a car or not. And then the money wouldn't go for roads and bridges. It would go for welfare; it would go for schools and everything else. So what do *you* think is a better deal?"

– 1991

■ ■ ■

When the Alaskan oil spill caused gasoline prices to increase, Cuomo ordered his state energy commissioner and the Consumer

Protection Board to launch an investigation. The governor warned that if evidence turned up that showed major oil companies were "acting in concert to exploit" the tragic spill, he would push for federal intervention.

"It would be patently unfair if the oil industry took advantage of a tragedy of its own making in Alaska as an excuse to increase retail gasoline prices. That would be the equivalent of picking the pockets of New York and American consumers."

– 1989

■ ■ ■

... ON HEALTH ISSUES

In the late 1980s, New York state had the most number of confirmed AIDS cases in the nation. Cuomo unveiled a five-year blueprint aimed at controlling the disease, but in outlining his plan, the governor admitted it did not go far enough. Nevertheless, the plan called for improving counseling services, enhancing outreach efforts and setting up education programs.

"New York State now has one out of every four AIDS cases in the country. It is essential that we confront the challenge of AIDS with all of our best instinct and talent."

– 1989

■ ■ ■

Health concerns were raised in the late 1980s when the state decided to let people move back into Love Canal, the nation's most infamous toxic waste site. Opponents of the controversial resettlement complained that Cuomo's silence on the issue was deafening. They pushed unsuccessfully to try to get the governor to overturn state Health Commissioner David Axelrod's decision to let people resettle part of the canal area in Niagara Falls.

Lois Gibbs, the former Love Canal housewife who vaulted into the national spotlight by leading the initial Love Canal revolt in the late 1970s, warned Cuomo that he was putting his national reputation on the line.

"It's morally wrong, there is no scientific evidence that it's safe, and he's putting women of reproductive age at risk," Gibbs contended.

– 1989

Love Canal homeowner Emmett Berard discusses his concerns with Cuomo following a meeting between state officials and Love Canal area residents. At left is Henry Williams, who headed the state Department of Environmental Conservation. Love Canal is the nation's most infamous toxic waste site.

■ ■ ■

... ON THE MIDDLE CLASS

Speaking to the National Press Club, Cuomo argued that even working class people who have managed to escape poverty have not escaped economic hardship.

"Middle class people are the people who are not poor enough to be on welfare and not rich enough to be worry-free. They're people who work for a living. Not because some psychiatrist tells them it's a convenient way to fill the grim interval between birth and eternity... they **have** to work for a living."

$-$ 1990

... ON QUESTION-DODGING

The governor is a master communicator who sometimes skillfully evades questions that he doesn't wish to address. His strategies are often employed during his monthly radio call-in show. For example, when the show's host asked a rather lengthy, two-pronged question, Cuomo responded:

"Well, let me start with the second part (of your question), and then maybe by the time I'm finished answering that, you'll forget the first part!"

$-$ 1991

When a caller asked the governor an extraordinarily detailed question about state automobile inspection procedures, Cuomo answered it this way:

"Louis, I want to congratulate you. I have very seldom been so totally stumped by the nice complexity of a question as I am at this moment."

$-$ 1991

Another caller was very critical of Cuomo, and he made no effort to hide his disdain. The governor ended the conversation by saying:

"You have this nice capacity for saying other people fudge when they disagree (with you). The next time you call, John, I wish you would just have a little bit of happiness in your voice!"

$-$ 1991

... ON RELIGION

"Even at the center of theology, probably the best thing you can do in life is function, experience, act. God gave you the capacity to exist. He doesn't want you to spend your time sleeping. He wants you to function. If you can function doing things that are good for other people, what can be better in life?"

-1985

■ ■ ■

Referring to his speech titled "Religious Belief & Public Morality, A Catholic Governor's Perspective," Cuomo underscored the difficulty of the issue:

"It's not easy to stay contained. Certainly, although everybody talks about a wall of separation between church and state. I've seen religious leaders scale that wall with all the dexterity of an Olympic athlete. In fact, I've seen so many candidates in churches and synagogues that I think we should change election day from Tuesdays to Saturdays or Sundays."

-1984

■ ■ ■

"I protect my right to be a Catholic by preserving your right to believe as a Jew, a Protestant or non-believer, or as anything else you choose. We know that the price of seeking to force our beliefs on others is that they might someday force theirs on us."

-1984

■ ■ ■

..."The Catholic church is my spiritual home. My heart is here and my hope."

-1984

■ ■ ■

While criss-crossing the campaign trail, Cuomo recalled a conversation he had with a UPI reporter while riding on a private plane.

..."We were talking about the Apostle's creed and heaven and hell when the plane was suddenly jolted by an air pocket. I think it was an air pocket - I hope it wasn't that (God) didn't like what we were saying about the Apostle's Creed."

-1982

■■■

... ON THE SAVINGS & LOAN SCANDAL

In his 1990 nomination speech, the governor told Democrats he was going to avoid talking about the savings and loan debacle because "then they'll say that's Washington bashing, and I don't want any Washington bashing."

But he later went on to discuss the scandal.

"These geniuses, these conservatives who believed that what you have to do is deregulate. Take these regulations off. Let these bankers do what they want to do. What did they do? They stole everything in sight and now you're paying for it."

Cuomo's attack brought the 350 party delegates to their feet.

- 1990

■■■

... ON SENATE ETHICS

When U.S. Senator Alfonse D'Amato found himself facing allegations of influence peddling, Cuomo defended the Republican representative.

"As soon as he gets vindicated, he'll go up so fast, so far, it'll change everything."

Did that mean Cuomo was presuming D'Amato would be cleared of any wrong-doing by congressional investigators?

"I hope he will be... He's my senator. What do you hope? (That) he gets convicted of something?"

Senate investigators ultimately cleared D'Amato of the charges.

■ ■ ■

... ON SMOKING

The governor at one time was a three-pack-a-day cigarette smoker. But in 1990, anti-smoking crusaders found a friend in Cuomo when he pushed for a ban on the sale of cigarettes from vending machines, except in bars or tobacco shops.

"Considering that the majority of smokers started before their 18th birthday, it is particularly important that we do everything possible to discourage young people from this potentially deadly habit."

– 1990

■ ■ ■

"Making cigarettes and other tobacco products less accessible to minors would be a significant step."

– 1990

■ ■ ■

... ON STATE GOVERNMENT

Cuomo once proposed borrowing a page from the British Parliament, where he would answer state lawmakers' inquiries during a regularly-scheduled "question hour." Anyone who has watched CNN knows that in Britian, the prime minister faces such an interrogation each week in the Parliament.

"How about a question hour in the Assembly and the Senate involving the governor? I'm for it... Governors ought to do that. They could call you names and do whatever you wanted to do and put it all on televison."

– 1990

■ ■ ■

"You know why it's so hard for people to think about the

accomplishments of the Cuomo administration? Because there are **so many** of them... My aides told me to concentrate on something. Pick one or two areas – be the Education Governor, be the Infrastructure Governor. But why? For political purposes? I wouldn't do it. But take a look at what we've done. I'm very, very proud of our record."

– 1990

■ ■ ■

... ON THE STOCK MARKET SCANDAL

When the insider trading scandal vaulted into the national spotlight, Cuomo voiced his views on the subject.

"It's particularly distressing to see people who make hundreds of millions of dollars, who park their Porsches next to their Maseratis, next to their Jaguars and don't know where to put their jacuzzi's, have to rip you off more."

– 1987

■ ■ ■

... ON SURROGATE PARENTING

Governor Cuomo urged lawmakers to pass a bill banning paid surrogate parenting contracts. He wrote the following message to the Legislature:

"Surrogate parenting for money is the selling of babies... The gestation of children as a service for others in exchange for a fee is a radical departure from the way in which society understands and values pregnancy."

– 1988

■ ■ ■

... ON UNITY

During a hearing on Capitol Hill, Cuomo gave congressmen his views on national unity.

"Is it right that the residents of New Jersey spend their money to subsidize farmers in Iowa? Why do Iowans contribute to mass transit in New Jersey? Why do the people of Alabama help build dams in the Northwest... A central idea at the heart of the republic (is) that we are one nation, not 50 nations, and that we are strongest when we stand together and help each other out."

– 1985

■ ■ ■

... ON VALUES

"When you have kids in elementary school and you don't teach anything about values, I suspect the message you're sending is that there are no values. What's happened in the last 20 years is that we've said 'No values – we'll teach no values.' It's all produced a vacuum. I don't think we're teaching any moral structure in any formal way."

– 1986

■ ■ ■

... ON VETERANS

Ask veterans what they think of New York's governor and you are likely to get two different answers. Some view Cuomo as an aggressive advocate for veterans, championing such measures as the state's veterans' bill of rights which was adopted in 1988. Others claim the governor's actions have fallen far short of his promises. In fact, when the Vietnam Veterans of America met in San Francisco and gave Cuomo an award, some vets from New York complained.

But over the years, the governor has vigorously defended his administration's track record when it comes to advancing the issues that are important to veterans.

"We have a very, very aggressive agenda of efforts and accomplishments for the Vietnam vets that we have been congratulated and thanked for over and over. I'm satisfied that we have done the right thing by Vietnam veterans."

– 1987

■ ■ ■

... ON WEALTH

"The (Reagan) administration says it wants to cut taxes to give people an incentive to work harder. Apparently in its view, the rich are so much lazier, that they need an incentive 60 times larger than most of you."

- 1985

■ ■ ■

... ON WELFARE

During a get-out-of-the-vote speech to supporters in Western New York, Cuomo reflected on his family's humble beginnings. He talked about his mother's perceptions of these tough times.

"She says she was never on welfare. I have these wonderful fights with her.

'I was never on welfare," she'll say.

Ma! Don't you remember when papa was a ditch digger and you were on relief?

'Oh, relief, ya. But never welfare!'

- 1990

■ ■ ■

"We have more single-parent families than ever before. More women in poverty. More teenage mothers without a proper education or the prospect of a job. We have increasing numbers of children whose mental and physical development have already been stunted by poor nutrition and inadequate medical care... At the same time we've heard (from the Reagan administration) a symphony of noble words about the reverence for life, we've seen savage cuts in the programs that help mothers and fathers sustain their children, that educate the young, that prevent birth defects."

- 1985

■ ■ ■

INDEX

About the Authors

Brian Meyer is Managing Editor of News at WBEN Radio in Buffalo where he has worked since 1982. He has won numerous state and regional awards for his coverage of local government, the criminal justice system and environmental issues.

A former president of the local chapter of the Society of Professional Journalists, Meyer writes for several local newspapers and hosts a weekly business show on cable television. The Buffalo native attended P.S. #56, St. Joseph's Collegiate Institute and Marquette University. He graduated with a journalism degree, minoring in marketing.

Meyer enjoys canoeing, hiking and swimming in the Allegany County town of Rushford, where he has a summer home.

Photo by Cathy Linden

Mary Murray is a producer for WIVB, a Buffalo television station. She specializes in investigative and consumer reporting.

Before acquiring a Bachelor of Science Degree in communications from Medaille College in Buffalo, Murray was certified by New York State as a Licensed Practical Nurse.

Murray lives in West Seneca, a Buffalo suburb, with her son, Kevin.

Western New York Wares, Inc.

Quotable Cuomo: The Mario Years – Hundreds of lively quotes from one of America's most effective public speakers are included in this book. Compiled by Brian Meyer and Mary Murray, the book contains more than a dozen photographs of Mario Cuomo and includes a comprehensive index. The consummate quote book for Cuomo fans and foes. **$5.95**

Hometown Heroes: Western New Yorkers in Desert Storm – More than one hundred people were interviewed, their experiences woven together in an enlightening text that affords a unique glimpse of Desert Storm. Written by Brian Meyer and Tom Connolly, this is not a book about war. Rather, it's a book about people and how their lives were touched by Desert Storm. **$5.95**

Designated Landmarks of the Niagara Frontier – About 100 landmarks spring to life in a fascinating look at the region's architectural past. Written by Austin Fox and illustrated by Lawrence McIntyre. **$13.95**

Symbol & Show: The Pan-American Exposition of 1901 – Written by Austin Fox and illustrated by Lawrence McIntyre, this book showcases one of Buffalo's most significant events. **$13.95**

Answers to the 100 Most Common Questions About Niagara Falls – Volunteer local falls historian Paul Gromosiak spent four summers at Niagara Falls, chatting with 40,000 tourists. This invaluable guide answers the most commonly asked questions. **$3.50**

Soaring Gulls and Bowing Trees: The History of the Islands Above Niagara Falls – Color photographs and insightful text focus on the magnetism and history of Niagara Falls. **$9.95**

Buffalo: A Bull's Eye View – Bizarre tales and quotes offer a humorous look at Western New York. This offbeat almanac contains 600 anecdotes and illustrations. **$4.95**

The Cheap Gourmets' Dining Guide to the Niagara Frontier (Now in its third edition!) – Doug and Polly Smith visit more than 50 restaurants. The eateries are categorized as "Very Cheap," "Pretty Cheap" and "Not Cheap at All." **$5.95**

Buffalo Bluff – A game of cunning hometown deception where players try to trick opponents by creating lies about local people, places and events. **$13.95**

Buffalo Chips (The Book) – Popular local cartoonist Tom Stratton has penned more than 100 humorous cartoons and essays in this 144-page book. **$6.95**

Sing a Song of Six-Packs – Buffalo politics is set to music in hilarious song parodies that focus on the feisty reign of Mayor Jimmy Griffin. Cassette tape and illustrated book. **$11.95**

Western New York Trivia Quotient – Crammed with 1,300 questions about the region. Fun and educational. **$7.95**

Buffalo's Waterfront: A Guidebook – Filled with drawings and maps, this fascinating armchair tour of the region's shoreline was edited by Tim Tielman and published by the Preservation Coalition of Erie County. More than 100 waterfront sites are showcased. **$5.95**

Please include 8% sales tax and $1 for shipping/handling costs. Send orders to:

Western New York Wares Inc.
P.O. Box 733
Ellicott Station
Buffalo, New York 14205

About the Publisher

Western New York's most innovative publishing company sprouted its roots in trivial turf.

The year was 1984 and the trivia craze was taking the nation by storm. Four friends sat in a North Buffalo living room playing one of the more popular games. Brian Meyer casually remarked that someone should concoct a trivia game that focused on Buffalo-area people, places and events. Several months later, *Western New York Trivia Quotient* was born. The game sold out its first edition in less than seven weeks.

One year later, Meyer came up with the notion of compiling a book of quotations that chronicled the unpredictable utterings of Buffalo's feisty mayor. *The World According to Griffin* was a popular stocking-stuffer during the 1985 holiday season.

Meyer Enterprises has published more than a dozen books and games that focus on hometown happenings. Among the most popular titles: *The Cheap Gourmets' Dining Guide to the Niagara Frontier* (currently in its third edition), *Niagara Falls Q & A* (also in its third printing), *Designated Landmarks of the Niagara Frontier* and *Buffalo: A Bull's Eye View.* During its first six years in existence, the company sold more than 35,000 copies of its Buffalo-oriented books and games.

More than 125 public libraries and schools have turned to these local publications for resource materials on Western New York's rich history.

Meyer Enterprises became Western New York Wares, Inc. in 1989. The company's most impressive growth pattern was logged in 1991 when it began diversifying its product mix and expanding its distribution network beyond the Niagara Frontier.

"This was the year in which the corporation stopped viewing challenges as obstacles and started viewing them as exciting opportunities," said Brian Meyer.

The publishing company has plans for developing no fewer than 15 new products over the next five years.